GET LOST

Get Lost

In the ancient trackways of the Lake District and Cumbria

Alan Cleaver & Lesley Park

Chitty Mouse Press

2020

Credits:

Published by Alan Cleaver and Lesley Park
Chitty Mouse Press, 57 Church Street,
Whitehaven, Cumbria CA28 7EX
Email: alanjcleaver@gmail.com
Website: https://sites.google.com/site/
alancleaverbooks/

Our thanks to:
Whitehaven Archive & Local Studies Centre,
pixabay.com; www.geog.port.ac.uk, David
Livermore, Martha Love, John Bainbridge,
Marianne Birkby, David Burbidge, Simon
Young, Tony Vaux, Mandy Lane, Sophia
Martin, Westmorland Shepherdess

First published January 2020

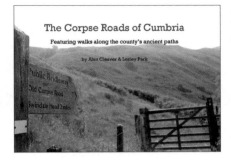

The Corpse Roads of Cumbria

Featuring walks along the county's ancient paths

by Alan Cleaver & Lesley Park

Also available:

THE CORPSE ROADS OF CUMBRIA:
These paths were used in medieval times to
carry the dead from rural parishes to the
'mother' church. Many still survive in Cumbria
as public footpaths. This book details their
routes, their history and the legends
surrounding them.

Front cover picture: The view from the
footpath above Beckfoot and looking east
along the Eskdale valley.

"Not all those who wander are lost"

– JRR Tolkien

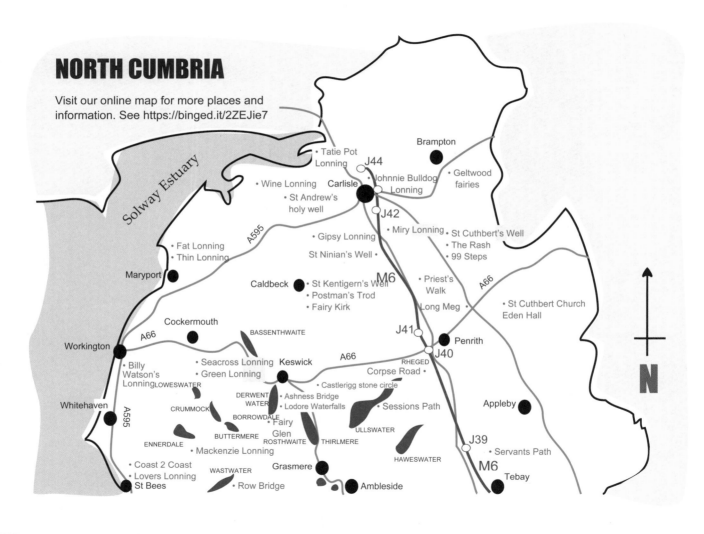

NORTH CUMBRIA

Visit our online map for more places and information. See https://binged.it/2ZEJie7

Solway Estuary

• Tatie Pot Lonning
J44
Carlisle
• Johnnie Bulldog Lonning
Brampton
• Geltwood fairies

• Wine Lonning
• St Andrew's holy well
J42

• Miry Lonning
• Gipsy Lonning
• St Cuthbert's Well
• The Rash
• 99 Steps

• Fat Lonning
• Thin Lonning

A595

• St Ninian's Well

M6

• Priest's Walk

A66

Maryport

Caldbeck
• St Kentigern's Well
• Postman's Trod
• Fairy Kirk

• Long Meg

• St Cuthbert Church Eden Hall

Cockermouth

BASSENTHWAITE

J41
Penrith

Workington

A66

A66

RHEGED
J40

• Seacross Lonning
Keswick
• Corpse Road

Appleby

• Billy Watson's Lonning
LOWESWATER
• Green Lonning

• Castlerigg stone circle

• Sessions Path

DERWENT WATER
• Ashness Bridge
• Lodore Waterfalls

Whitehaven

A595

CRUMMOCK

BORROWDALE

• Fairy Glen
ROSTHWAITE

ULLSWATER

J39

BUTTERMERE

THIRLMERE

• Servants Path

ENNERDALE

• Mackenzie Lonning

HAWESWATER

M6

• Coast 2 Coast
WASTWATER
Grasmere

Tebay

• Lovers Lonning
St Bees

• Row Bridge

• Ambleside

N

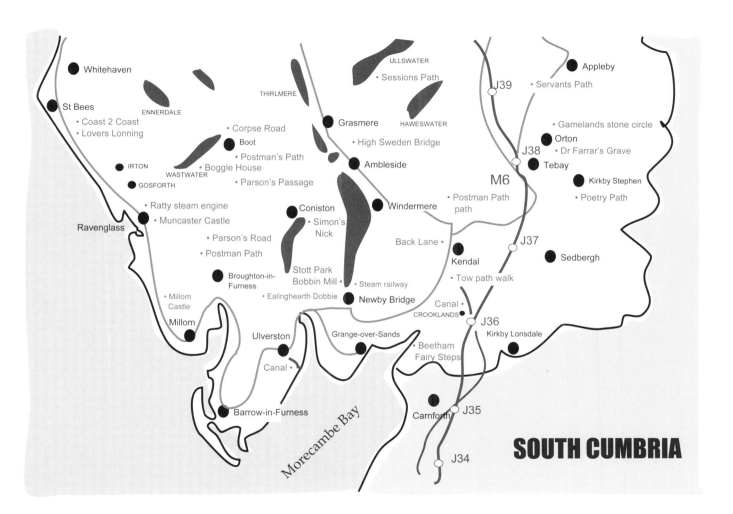

Whitehaven

St Bees
• Coast 2 Coast
• Lovers Lonning

ENNERDALE

IRTON

WASTWATER

GOSFORTH

Ravenglass

• Ratty steam engine
• Muncaster Castle

• Parson's Road

• Postman Path

Broughton-in-Furness

• Millom Castle

Millom

Ulverston

• Canal

Barrow-in-Furness

THIRLMERE

• Corpse Road

Boot

• Postman's Path

• Boggle House

• Parson's Passage

Coniston

• Simon's Nick

Stott Park Bobbin Mill

• Ealinghearth Dobbie

Newby Bridge

Grange-over-Sands

Carnforth

ULLSWATER

• Sessions Path

Grasmere

• High Sweden Bridge

Ambleside

HAWESWATER

Windermere

• Steam railway

Back Lane •

Kendal

• Tow path walk

Canal

CROOKLANDS

J36

• Beetham Fairy Steps

J35

J34

Morecambe Bay

J39

• Servants Path

Appleby

• Gamelands stone circle

Orton
J38
• Dr Farrar's Grave

Tebay

Kirkby Stephen

• Poetry Path

M6

• Postman Path path

J37

Sedbergh

Kirkby Lonsdale

SOUTH CUMBRIA

Contents

Introduction

THE Lake District is the most visited national park in the UK and it's easy to see why. However, it is sometimes nice to find a spot away from the crowds. That's where this book comes in. *Get Lost* reveals the lonnings, trods and quieter footpaths throughout the Lake District and Cumbria that are usually only known to us locals; places of unpublicised beauty where you can find peace and quiet – and perhaps a bit of history to intrigue you. Not that we want to put you off visiting Ambleside, Coniston, Ashness Bridge, Scafell Pike or those other iconic locations. They are certainly worth visiting. But the Lake District is only part of the huge county of Cumbria and there is so much more to visit. We include locations in the national park but also encourage you to take a short journey beyond the boundaries to discover such delights as the Solway estuary, the Eden Valley, the coastline of west Cumbria or other enchanted spots. This book's title – *Get Lost* – is a play on words of course. We want you to get lost metaphorically in the beautiful landscape; to give your mind a break from the stresses of city life and the modern world as you walk down a lonning. But we don't want

GET LOST

1

you to literally get lost so have included maps, detailed routes and grid references. If you do find yourself where you shouldn't be, then see the chapter *Don't Get Lost* on page 168 for some advice on navigation. For the most part, however, our walks are low-level, short and family friendly. We particularly favour those with a nearby cafe or pub.

Cumbria seems to delight in a rich vocabulary for its paths. There are lonnings, trods, drovers roads, corpse roads, waths, rakes, meanderings, packhorse routes and many other types of path. And then they

often have specific names, often only known to the local villagers. Hence you will find Johnnie Bulldog Lonning, Chitty Mouse Path, the Ninety-nine Steps, Bloody Bones Lane or the

Pitman's Trod. Some reflect the nature of the path; others relate to the history of the area but the origin of most are lost to us. All the paths we describe are public footpaths but you are unlikely to find the names listed by Ordnance Survey or Google. They are 'secrets' waiting to be discovered. Each has its own characteristics but all should be walked at a slow, slare, pace (see page 8). There is much to see if only you take the time to stand still and look more carefully. Stand still even for a short time and the hitherto hidden birds and wildlife will start to peek their heads out from the bushes.

Finally, to properly immerse you in the culture of Cumbria we

Nanny Knockabouts near
Cumwhinton. The lonning is
so named because children
played there after school
Grid Ref: NY455 533.

GET
LOST
3

have included some dialect words. Don't panic. We also include a glossary of these and other 'lost words' on page 171. We feel it is important to help promote the local language as much as the local landscape. For those who wish to learn more, we recommend visiting the website of the Lakeland Dialect Society.

Throughout the book we give grid references and post codes. You can type these into the website gridreferencefinder.com which will show you precisely where they are on an OS map.

T'Crack: One of the narrow alleyways to be found in Kendal. Grid Ref: SD515 920.

A lesson for us all

"It is not down in any map; true places never are"

— Herman Melville

AMERICAN Elihu Burritt (1810 to 1879) loved walking and the longer the walk the better. In 1863 he came to England to walk from Essex to Land's End. His first day of walking from Tiptree to Coggeshall went well but the second day ended disastrously with him getting hopelessly lost. Not that he realised his error straight away. Here he describes what happened after the landlady at his lodgings at Great Bardfield put him on the path to Saffron Walden. It is a warning to all those who are absolutely convinced they are *not* lost:

"After giving me minute directions as to the course I was to follow, she bade me goodbye, and I proceeded on at a brisk pace through fields of wheat and clover, greatly enjoying the scenery, the air and exercise. Soon I came to a large field quite recently ploughed up clean, footpath and all. Seeing a gate at each of the opposite corners, I made my way across the furrows to the one at the left, as it seemed to be more in the direction indicated by my host. There the path was again broad and well-trodden, and I followed it through many fields of grain yellowing to the harvest, until it opened into the main road. This bore a little more to the left than I expected but as I had never travelled it before, I believed it was all right. Thaxted was half way to Saffron Walden and there I had intended to stop an hour or two for dinner and rest, then push on to the end of the day's walk as

Marking the way: Watch out for ancient milestones that still survive by the roadsides in Cumbria.

speedily as possible. At about noon, I came suddenly down upon the town, which seemed remarkably similar to the one I had left, in size, situation and general features. The parish church also bore a strong resemblance to the one I had noticed the previous evening. These old Essex towns are 'as much alike as two peas' and you must make a note of it, as Captain Cuttle says, was the thought first suggested by the coincidence. I went into a cosy, clean-faced inn on the main street, and addressed myself with much satisfaction to a short season of rest and refreshment, exchanging hot and dusty boots for slippers, and going through other preliminaries to make a comfortable time of it. I rang the bell for dinner, but before ordering it, asked the waiting-maid, with a complacent idea that I had improved my walking pace, and made more than half the way.

'How far is it to Saffron Walden?'
'Twelve miles, sir.'
'Twelve miles indeed! Why, it is only twelve miles from Great Bardfield!'
'Well this is Great Bardfield, sir.'
'Great Bardfield! What! How is this? What do you mean?'

She meant what she said, and it was as true as two and two make four; and she was not to be beaten out of it by a state of astonishment, however a discomfitted man might expand his eyes with wonder, or cloud his face with chagrin. It was a patent fact. There, on the opposite side of the street, was the house in which I slept the night before; and here, just coming up to the door of the inn, was the good lady of my host. Her form and voice, and other identifications dispelled the mist of the mistake; and it came out as clear as day that I had followed the direction of my host, to bear to the left, far too liberally, and that I had been walking at my best speed in a 'vicious circle' for full two hours and a half, and had landed just where I commenced, at least within the breadth of a narrow street of the same point."

An old milestone near Gosforth – but one that is in desperate need of a lick of paint.

To slare — to walk with no particular purpose

THERE is an old Cumbrian dialect word – slare – which means to walk slowly, to amble, to walk with no particular purpose. It is the perfect word to describe the pace at which lonnings, trods and other paths should be walked. Take your time walking. Every now and again stop. If you just wait quietly for a few minutes you will hopefully see wildlife which you may have otherwise missed. Too often people are rushing. There is a modern craze to 'do things in 24 hours' or in a record time. The Lake District has a number of events that encourage participants to race as fast as they can on bike or foot. The 'Three Peakers' attempt to climb Ben Nevis, Scafell Pike and Snowdon in 24 hours. These are the highest mountains of Wales, England and Scotland. When they arrive at Wasdale Head they dash up Scafell Pike and a few hours later – having 'done' the peak – speed off to Snowdon in Wales. They have, of course, not 'done' Scafell Pike or the other peaks at all. They have not seen the mountains or the valleys. Ask them to name a bird or flower they have seen and they won't be able to tell you. They've achieved precious little other than upsetting the local people and the landscape. When you slare down a lonning you begin to appreciate the delicate natural world it contains, begin to see how it has evolved over the centuries and hear what it has to say about man and the landscape he inhabits.

See also Lost Words on p171.

GET LOST

8

A way with the fairies

*"The fault of the present age is, not that it believes too much,
but that it believes too little"*

— Robert Anderson, 1805

THERE is perhaps a surprising number of fairy legends in Cumbria – creatures you might more commonly associate with Cornwall, Devon, Ireland or even the Isle of Man. But as late as the 19th Century there was a strong belief in fairies in Cumberland and Westmorland (the two counties merged to form Cumbria in 1974). Nineteenth century authors such as Jeremiah Sullivan, William Henderson and Robert Anderson seemed to recognise that the gradual encroachment of modern ways would soon wipe away the last vestiges of these wonderful creatures who for so many centuries had lived side by side with us mortals. The writers were quick to tell their more educated London readers that only the simplest of rural folk still believed in such things — but then lost little time describing the intricate details of the fairies, boggles and goblins down to the colour of their coat, what they ate and how

GET LOST
9

best to approach them. Do not think of the Walt Disney Tinkerbell-type of fairy with gossamer wings. English fairies were traditionally just slightly smaller than the human race and in many cases lived happily alongside their human neighbours.

John Briggs, a former editor of *The Westmorland Gazette*, had a number of his letters and papers published in 1825 and in them he talks with authority about ghosts, dobbies, witches and the like. But he is one of a number of writers who declared that fairies **were** no more:

GET LOST
10

"Fairies which were once so plentiful in this

Gelt Wood Fairies

Most years, fairy doors have appeared each summer (June to September) in trees and hedges around Gelt Wood, near Brampton (see picture opposite). They're a joy to see but we won't reveal here the precise location out of respect for the neighbours. Email us and we'll advise if they are currently there and send you a precise map: alanjcleaver@gmail.com

country are completely gone. Even those who believe they once existed acknowledge they are now extinct. They were a race of beings between

men and spirits. They had marriages and reared children, followed occupations and particularly churned their own butter. Their habitations were in caves and they were considered perfectly harmless, capable of being visible or invisible at pleasure and generally of small stature. We have never been able to learn whether they were immortal or not or whether they were liable to future rewards or punishments."

But as we will discover, Mr Briggs may have been too quick to write off our fairy neighbours. We cannot guarantee you will see any fairies during your visit to Cumbria but we can hopefully point you in the direction of some magical places

One of the fairy doors that appears most years near Gelt Wood, Brampton.

GET LOST
11

associated with legends of the fairy folk and the county can even provide hard evidence of their existence in the shape of a glass goblet stolen from the fairies.

THE Luck of Eden Hall was snatched from the fairies by the butler of Eden Hall and was for many years in the possession of the Musgrave family near Penrith. It is now in the safe keeping of the Victoria and Albert Museum in London. And there's good reason for wanting to keep it safe: According to tradition if the goblet ever breaks the good fortune of Eden Hall will come to an end. The tale

GET LOST

12

Made by fairies: The remarkable Luck of Eden Hall, a crystal goblet 'snatched from the fairies' seen dancing at Eden Hall, Cumbria. Picture courtesy of the Victoria & Albert Museum.

tells how the butler of Eden Hall, went to the nearby St Cuthbert's Well for some water and came upon fairies dancing there. This lovely object was in their midst and, drawn by its beauty, he reached over and grabbed it. The fairies put up a struggle, but it was in vain. As they fled they uttered the now famous warning:

"If this glass shall break or fall, then farewell the luck of Eden Hall"

There is a tale that in the 17th Century, Sir Christopher Musgrave did accidentally drop the goblet – but before it could smash on the floor it was caught in a napkin by the butler. Several lucks are associated with

PENRITH, FAIRY WELL, EDENHALL.

A 20th Century postcard of St Cuthbert's Well, Eden Hall – the well is now on private land but you can visit St Cuthbert's Church.

Cumbrian houses and families, and some have attracted similar legends but none of the lucks are as beautiful as the Eden Hall goblet. And for once the more prosaic explanation for the origins of the Luck of Eden Hall does not detract from its truly magical qualities. According to experts, it was made in Egypt or Syria in the 13th Century, and presumably brought back to the wilds of Cumbria by a crusader after many years in the Near East. But the technology needed to make clear glass was unknown in northern Europe at that time, and the skill needed to enamel such a fragile object must have seemed magical.

GET LOST

13

Undoubtedly the legend which grew around the Luck of Eden Hall helped to preserve it for 700 years. And that is something we can all thank the fairies for. St Cuthbert's Well, mentioned in the legend, is on private land but you can visit St Cuthbert's Church and there are many fairy sites in the county you can visit.

THE Borrowdale valley, south of Keswick, is home to a number of fairy legends, including a picturesque Fairy Glen which we recommend as a family walk. This beautiful valley is also home to the hobthross, a most unusual breed of fairy. He was (or is) a house

Fairy Glen, Borrowdale.

fairy who would live by the fire and help the household with menial tasks. As one 19th Century writer described him:

"In the day time he lurked in remote recesses of the old houses which he delighted to haunt; and in the night, sedulously employed himself in discharging any laborious task which he thought might be acceptable to the family, to whose service he had devoted himself. He loved to stretch himself by the kitchen fire when the menials had taken their departure. Before the glimpse of morn he would execute more work than could be done by a man in ten days."

He might wash the dishes or bring in the corn or other tasks.

The hobthross.

There was just one 'rule' – you must never reward a hobthross for his good works or he would pack his bags and leave. The most you could give him was a mess of milk porridge left out for him by the fire. The story

tells how a maid saw him one winter's night crossing the yard outside and felt sorry for him in his poor attire so she made him a new coat with a hood. The next day, the hobthross left the farm declaring:

"Hob has got a new coat and new hood, And Hob no more will do any good."

A similar story is told of a hobthross who once lived at Millom Castle.

Fairy Glen is the local name for Galleny Force, a beauty spot on Stonethwaite Beck at the end of the Borrowdale Valley. It's a good walk for families and

GET LOST

15

Watendlath: Where you'll find this charming packhorse bridge and a tea room.

the Fairy Glen itself is an ideal spot for a picnic. And it may just be coincidence but it was near this glen that two ladies claimed to have seen a group of fairies in 1941 after getting lost on the fell above Rosthwaite. In *Seeing Fairies* by Marjorie T Johnson the two ladies – Miss Nora M Best and Miss Agnes Robson – told how they spotted what they believed to be the 'Little People' somewhere between Rosthwaite and Watendlath, en route to Dock Tarn. The odds of seeing the fairies again may be remote but it's certainly a worthy walk with a tea room at either end.

GET LOST 16

You can start in the village of Rosthwaite with tea at the Flock Inn tea rooms or one of the other hostelries in the village. There are also public toilets near the Flock Inn. Head north out of the village and then take the path on your right which will lead you up the fell to the village of Watendlath. It was somewhere near the brow of this hill that the fairies were seen. To quote Marjorie T Johnson in *Seeing Fairies: "Suddenly they heard the shrill laughter of children, and, about a hundred yards below them, they saw what they thought were four or five children scampering about each other round two or three rather big boulders. Thinking that there must be a track near, the two companions immediately made a beeline for the spot, quite expecting to find a family party on the other side of the boulders. But when they arrived, no one was there, and although they searched around for a considerable time, calling 'Coo-ee' there was nothing to be seen or heard. They were more than a little mystified. 'We realised,' they said, 'that it was an unlikely place for children to be in and, as we had reached the spot in two or three minutes after seeing them, there was no place to which they could*

have disappeared. Comparing impressions, we both had seen what we thought were small children with long hair streaming out behind them as they ran and a general look of quaintness about them. We have been puzzled ever since. Could we have disturbed the Little People at their play? We wonder!'."

Staying with fairies

YOU can stay in a house reputedly lived in by a fairy. Legend tells how a fairy at Moresby Hall near Whitehaven guards buried treasure. If you are a true descendant of the Druids who buried the treasure you can approach the fountain that magically appears at the

Hall once a year and claim the treasure. The fairy is said to be in the form of a swan who floats on the lake created by the fountain.

Gnome alone

Wastwater in west Cumbria has a 'gnome garden' at the bottom of the lake. It was set up by divers who practise in the lake. Sadly you can't see it unless you are a diver but this valley is also 'Britain's Favourite View' which has to be a satisfactory consolation prize.

GET LOST

17

Borrowdale Fairy Path

THE walk to the Fairy Glen is an easy family walk but if you are intending to follow the path Miss Best and Miss Robson took when they encountered their fairies you will need to be prepared for a steep climb and a tough walk. But your reward is afternoon tea at the Caffle House tea room at Watendlath.

It confuses some tourists that there is no village of Borrowdale to find on the map; Borrowdale is the name of the valley and its principal village is Rosthwaite. You can catch the bus from Keswick down the valley or even

the boat to Grange. If you drive there are a number of parking options including a National Trust car park, an honesty-box car park at the village hall or hotels that offer public parking for a small fee. Our favoured option is the Borrowdale School where you know putting money in their honesty box helps support them.

You reach the footpath (Cumbria Way) to the fairy glen by counter-intuitively heading north out of Rosthwaite and take the first road on the right which leads you to a bridge and turn right onto the footpath. Follow this all the way to Galleny Force

(the proper name for Fairy Glen). It runs alongside Stonethwaite Beck. If you have parked at Borrowdale School you can take the path on the opposite side of the river.

Double back to then take the path up the side of the valley, past Dock Tarn to Watendlath. You can complete a circular route by dropping down from Watendlath to Rosthwaite. We enjoy the Flock Inn tea room at Rosthwaite but there are other eateries in the village. Nearby are the Bowder Stone, Borrowdale Yews and Lodore Falls.

GET LOST

18

THE precise location of the sighting of the 'Little People' by Miss Nora M Best and Miss Agnes Robson is unknown but it would have been around the top of the path leading from Stonethwaite to Dock Tarn. Be aware it is a steep climb.

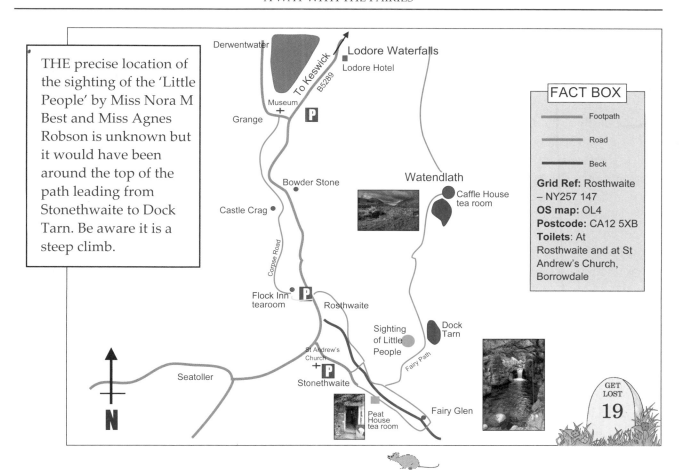

Derwentwater

To Keswick

B5289

Lodore Waterfalls

Lodore Hotel

Museum

Grange

P

Bowder Stone

Watendlath

Caffle House tea room

Castle Crag

Corpse Road

Flock Inn tearoom

P

Rosthwaite

Sighting of Little People

Dock Tarn

Fairy Path

St Andrew's Church

P

Seatoller

Stonethwaite

Peat House tea room

Fairy Glen

N

FACT BOX

Footpath

Road

Beck

Grid Ref: Rosthwaite – NY257 147
OS map: OL4
Postcode: CA12 5XB
Toilets: At Rosthwaite and at St Andrew's Church, Borrowdale

GET LOST

19

Simon's Nick, Coniston

CLIMB out of the beautiful village of Coniston in the south of the Lake District and head towards Levers Water. Beside there you will see some deep mine workings including the peculiarly-named Simon's Nick. Who was Simon? He was a copper miner in the mid-19th Century when digging for this precious metal was a major industry in the Coniston area. And he was a friend of the fairies. Legend has it that he befriended the fairies in the area and they were happy to tell him where to dig to find the rich veins of copper – on condition that he never told anyone of their existence. For years, Simon reaped the benefit of this deal but one day he had a bit too much to drink and finally told friends about the helping hand he received from the fairies. His 'deal' broken with the little folk, Simon's good fortune ran dry and he later died in an accident with the explosives used for mining.

VISITING SIMON'S NICK

Head out of the village past the Black Bull Inn and follow the signs to the Coppermines Youth Hostel. You will eventually reach Levers Water. This was a natural tarn but it was dammed and enlarged to provide power

Simon's Nick.

for the coppermine workers. Beside the Water you will see the mine workings including Simon's Nick.

GET LOST
20

A WAY WITH THE FAIRIES

Last of the fairies

FAIRIES were spotted around 1750 by a Jack Wilson of Martindale. He was crossing the fell near Sandwick when he saw fairies dancing in the moonlight. Jeremiah Sullivan retold the story in 1857 in his book, *Cumberland and Westmorland Ancient and Modern*: "He drew near unobserved, and presently described a stee (ladder) reaching from amongst them up into a cloud. But no sooner was the presence of a mortal discovered than all made a hasty retreat up the stee. Jack rushed forward, doubtless firmly determined to follow them into fairy-land, but arrived too late. They had affected their retreat,

Beetham Fairy Steps

There is a fairy path from Silverdale to Beetham (near Milnthorpe) which incorporates some magical fairy steps (pictured). If you can squeeze through the gap in the rock without touching the sides you will be granted your wish! The route is also an old corpse road.

Grid Ref: SD486 789

and quickly drawing up the stee, they shut the cloud and disappeared."

Today this reads more like a UFO encounter with the fairies climbing a ladder into a 'cloud'.

Sandwick is on the shores of Ullswater (Grid Ref: NY421 195). Rigg is an old term for a 'ridge'.

GET LOST

21

Caldbeck

ONE fairy walk we can highly recommend is from the picturesque village of Caldbeck (Grid Ref: NY320 399). You can park in the village where there are a number of pubs, cafes or places to picnic. Then it's a short walk along the river to the Fairy Kettle and the Fairy Kirk. We should start by saying that the term *kettle* refers to the swirling basin of water under a short waterfall – known as the Howk – on the Whelpo Beck as it hurtles through the valley. And *kirk* is an old Cumbrian word for church and refers to the adjacent cave where the fairies once met. It's a simple and pleasing walk for young and old members of the family. You can picnic by the river (the ruins of a bobbin mill can also be seen there) and enjoy the craft shops and eateries in the village too. One of the legends surrounding the Caldbeck fairies tells of a villager, Janet Wythburn, who fell in love with a man, married and had a child, only to discover later that her husband was one of the fairy race. Marriages between humans and fairies sadly rarely work out well! ■ See also p33.

GET LOST
22

The Fairy Kettle at Caldbeck.

The Sessions Trail

"The real hiker sees the by-ways and leafy lanes. He does not twang a mandolin, nor does he make the countryside hideous with ribald song"

– Arthur Sharp, 1934

MARTINDALE sits in the east of the county beneath Ullswater and is a sparsely populated area with farming and tourism the only 'industries' to be found there. But 200 years ago there was a thriving bobbin mill at Howtown; bobbins are wooden spindles used to hold wool or cotton. Although the mill has long gone, one legacy is the path that was used by the apprentice boys at the mill who would walk to St Martin's Church, Martindale. And thanks to the discovery of old music manuscripts in an attic, we even know the songs the boys sang.

John Wright found the manuscripts in his Martindale home around 2005 — they had belonged to his five-times great grandfather, John Jackson II. Jackson was the village schoolmaster and choirmaster. Mr Wright told the *Cumberland and Westmorland Herald*: "I found these old books and I didn't realise how important they were until I spoke with David Burbidge, who sings in a West Gallery choir. I am very keen for the music to be heard by people as it has been sitting hidden away for such a long time."

GET LOST
23

West Gallery choirs refers to the singers and musicians who performed in churches in the 18th and 19th Centuries. They sang in a gallery at the West End of the church. But by the end of the 19th Century the choirs were considered too 'rustic' and were dropped in favour of an organ and school children's choir. At Martindale the choir was dispensed with when a new church (St Peter's) complete with organ was built nearby. On the day it was opened, the roof of the old church fell in taking the West Gallery with it. The old church survives though and is well worth a visit. Beside it you will find

The interior of St Martin's church, Martindale. The gallery collapsed in 1880. The font is a Roman altar brought down from the nearby Roman road, High Street.

the famous Martindale yew trees believed to date back at least 700 years, suggestive of the fact that the site was used for worship long before the first record of a church there in the 13th Century.

A concert was held in 2007 performing the church's West Gallery music and sung by the Gladly Solemn Choir; you can find a video on YouTube.

GET LOST
24

SESSIONS TRAIL

GRADE: Easy with a good path but we recommend taking a map and knowing how to take a bearing. See page 169.

LENGTH: 2 kilometres each way.

TIME: Allow an hour each way.

CAFE: The Howtown Hotel bar and tea room on the main road.

TOILETS: At the Howtown Hotel cafe/bar

There is only limited parking at the Howtown end of Ullswater with more signs saying 'No Parking' than 'Parking'. So we

GET LOST 25

recommend the much more pleasant option of parking at Pooley Bridge or Glenridding and taking an Ullswater Steamer to Howtown. We can't imagine a nicer start (or finish) to a walk. When you come off the boat, turn right on the main road and a few yards further along take the first left. This track follows the beck that once drove the bobbin mill. There is a footpath by the beck but its start is sometimes overgrown so you can just take the main track. Follow this over a bridge and past some houses before turning left and uphill onto the fell. The beck will now be on your left.

St Martin's Church, Martindale with its famous yews.

After you have gone over the cattle grid, turn right following the sign-posted path. It is a short, steep climb before it levels out onto a terrace path that is well made and offers dramatic views over Ullswater. There are even a couple of seats along the path where you can stop to have your lunch. As you leave the lake behind, you'll pass The Coombs (a slight hill) on your right. You can turn right and look down upon (or even visit)

GET LOST
26

the new church of St Peter's, built in 1880 but we're going to bear left and continue to the old church. This is where you may get lost so pay attention. Bear left and on your right you will see a gate to go through. Once through that bear left and you will go round the crest of a hill a short distance to a house called Cotehow (pictured right). The path goes round the front of these delightful buildings before dropping down to the single-track road and on to St Martin's Church.

Enjoy a visit to the church before returning either by the same path or take the path to Sandwick (home to some fairies – see page 21) then follow the Ullswater Way footpath beside

The old school master's house (now private) is en route to St Martin's Church.

the lake back to Howtown. At Howtown you can reward yourself with tea (or something stronger) at the Howtown Hotel cafe/bar before taking the boat back to Pooley Bridge or Glenridding.

- Our thanks to David Burbidge, director of Lakeland Voice for his help with this chapter.

GET LOST
27

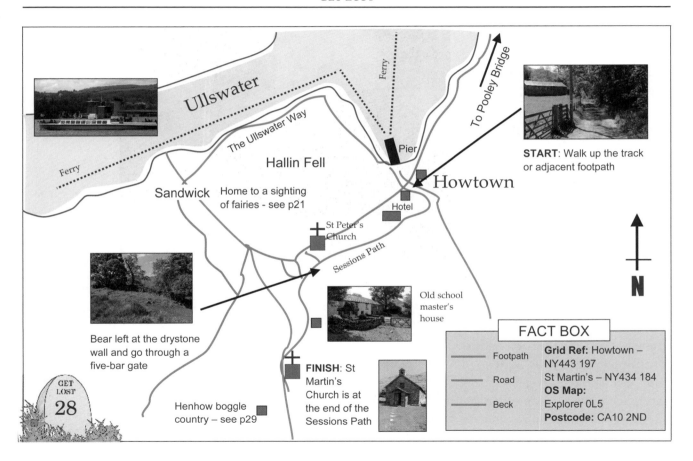

Ullswater

Ferry

Ferry

To Pooley Bridge

Pier

START: Walk up the track or adjacent footpath

The Ullswater Way

Hallin Fell

Home to a sighting of fairies - see p21

Howtown

Sandwich

Hotel

St Peter's Church

Sessions Path

Old school master's house

Bear left at the drystone wall and go through a five-bar gate

FINISH: St Martin's Church is at the end of the Sessions Path

Henhow boggle country – see p29

GET LOST 28

N

FACT BOX

──── Footpath	**Grid Ref:** Howtown – NY443 197
──── Road	St Martin's – NY434 184
──── Beck	**OS Map:** Explorer 0L5
	Postcode: CA10 2ND

On the path of the Henhow Boggle

JEREMIAH Sullivan, in his 1857 book, *Cumberland & Westmorland, Ancient and Modern* said even "incredulous individuals" who were sceptical of boggles (ghosts) would be swayed by the case of the Henhow Boggle at Martindale. He wrote:

"It happened about twenty-three years ago. The man to whom the boggle appeared was living in Martindale, at a cottage called Henhow. One morning he had to go to his work at an early hour, and having several miles to walk, he started soon after midnight. He had not got above two hundred yards from the house, when the dog by which he was accompanied, gave signs of alarm. He looked round – at the other side of the wall that bounded the road, appeared a woman, keeping pace with him, and carrying a child in her arms. There was no means of escape; he spoke to the figure, and asked her what "was troubling her?". Then she told him her story. She had once lived at Henhow, and had been seduced. Her seducer, to cloak his guilt and her frailty, met her by appointment at a certain market town, and gave her a medicine, the purpose of which is obvious. It proved too potent, and killed both mother and child. Her doom was to wander thus for a hundred years, forty of which were already expired. On his return home at night, the man told what he had seen and heard; and when the extraordinary story spread through the dale, the 'old wives' were able to recall some almost forgotten incidents precisely identical with those related by the boggle. The seducer was known to be a clergyman. The occurrence is believed to have made a lasting impression on the old man, who still lives, and was until very lately a shepherd on the fells."

GET LOST

29

Night Walking

WE know of no one these days who indulges in the lost art of Night Walking. Nor indeed are we regular practitioners. A hundred years ago, however, it was a popular pastime with participants declaring it was an effective way to ease stress and still the mind so perhaps it should be revived?

RW Hall devoted a chapter to Night Walking in his 1932 book, *The Art of Mountain Tramping*. Tramping is an archaic word for rambling. We quote what Mr Hall said

on the topic in the hopes it inspires you to try it out:

"If ordinary day walking has such charm, night walking has as great, if not greater. For the brain-tired man there is nothing more restful than strolling by moonlight or starlight for miles on what in daytime may be a monotonous road. The stars, 'silent above us', are more restful than anything I know. Starlight has a gentler influence than the jolly round face of 'Old Sol', much as we like him. To the man who for the first time walks by a silent lake in which the bright stars of winter are reflected, whilst on the hills above him the flaming stars appear to lie, there comes a sense of peace and beauty ever remembered. It will do no one any harm to walk a couple of hours beyond midnight, for, valuable as sleep is, there are other things of value."

He goes on to encourage readers to start Moonlight Rambling Clubs, walking from 10pm to 12pm on the night of a full moon. Now there's an idea…

The Postman's Trod

First class walks created by our postmen

NO matter how lost you are or how remote the spot you find yourself in, there will always be a postbox nearby. According to the Royal Mail, no one in Britain is ever more than three miles away from the iconic red postboxes that are so much a part of the British landscape. One wonders how much longer that will be in this digital age where, according to a 2015 survey, one third of teenagers have never written a letter. The early 20th Century heyday of the letter saw three or four deliveries a day and meant you could post a card to a friend in the morning to

GET LOST
31

advise you would call on them in the afternoon. The postal service may have slowed down a bit since then but when we're out walking we will usually write a postcard to our friends and drop it in the most remote postbox we can find. Can we encourage you to post a card or letter wherever you walk? If you're running low on friends, you can always send us a card to 57 Church Street, Whitehaven CA28 7EX.

There are a few postmen's trods in Cumbria — paths created by, or made popular by, the postman and this chapter celebrates these.

GET LOST
32

Caldbeck

SINCE it was author Tony Vaux at Caldbeck who introduced us to postman's paths, we'll start with a suggested walk around some of those surrounding Caldbeck. Tony, author of *Caldbeck: A Special Part of Lakeland*, points out, "the post paths between the farms were created after the walls had been built and are characterised by a lot of stiles (some of them requiring gymnastic feats) and field crossings at odd angles". So be warned. You may need to be reasonably athletic to climb over the drystone walls. We suggest parking in the beautiful village of Caldbeck (pictured right).

You may wish to start and finish your walk at Caldbeck's old post office and perhaps post a letter from there too.

GET LOST 33

This is a village remote enough to deter most tourists but that's a pity as it's stunningly beautiful with grand walks on the commons and fells. In the village there is also much to see including the church, a holy well, a spitting stone, a former mill (now home to an arts and crafts centre), a cafe, gift shops and pubs. There is even that most rare of features in the British landscape: public toilets.

You'll find a free car park (with honesty box) in Caldbeck's centre. From there it's a short walk via the exit up hill onto the common and towards the pond. The village's post office (Kirkland Stores) also make an ideal

The start of the path leading to Caldbeck's Postman Path.

start and finish point. Look for a footpath beside the large green hut; it goes through the yard of some houses but is clearly marked 'public footpath' (see picture above). It drops down to the Howk, a limestone gorge with an exhilarating race of water and including such features as the Fairy Kettle (a

whirlpool of water) and a Fairy Kirk. Kirk is dialect for church but this is actually a cave (see picture on next page). This is a beautiful wooded path beside the river. Ignore the bridge and continue west along Whelpo Beck until you reach Whelpo Bridge. Stay on the northern side of the beck and head on the farm

GET LOST
34

GET
LOST
35

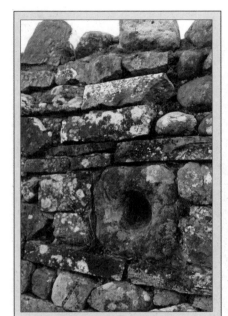

The Spitting Stone is set into a wall on the B5299 just outside Caldbeck. Tradition states if you spit in it on your way past and don't look back, your wishes will be granted! Grid Ref: NY322 396.

GET LOST 36

track towards Whelpo Head. Just beyond the drive to Whelpo Head turn right to join the postman's path as it heads up the hill to the first stile (there is a gate next to this one though). The path skirts past some woodland before reaching the corner of the field where you'll find the next stile. Keep the drystone wall on your right as you continue to head north and keep an eye out for a cleverly camouflaged stile in the drystone wall which will lead you over the field towards Brownrigg Farm. Cross this and you will see on the other side of Brownrigg's drive another stile in the wall. You will now need your wits about you and you'll benefit from taking a bearing with your map and compass (see

The steps over the drystone walls can sometimes be very well camouflaged.

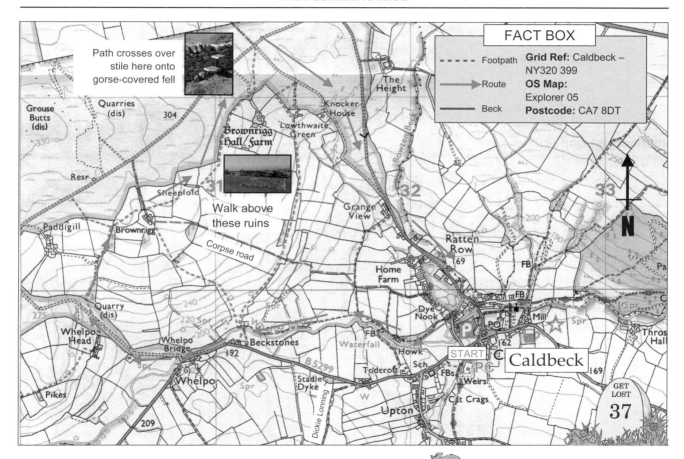

Path crosses over stile here onto gorse-covered fell

FACT BOX

– – –	Footpath	**Grid Ref:** Caldbeck – NY320 399
→	Route	**OS Map:** Explorer 05
───	Beck	**Postcode:** CA7 8DT

Grouse Butts (dis)

Quarries (dis)

304

Brownrigg Hall Farm

Lowthwaite Green

Knocker House

The Height

Bowten Beck

Resr

Sheepfold

Walk above these ruins

Paddigill

Brownrigg

Corpse road

Grange View

Ratten Row
169

FB

N

Home Farm

Quarry (dis)

Whelpo Head

Whelpo Bridge

Beckstones

Spr

Waterfall

Dye Nook

FB

Mill

Spr

Thros Hall

192

Spr

B 5299

Thowk

FBs

START

Caldbeck

169

Whelpo

Stadle Dyke

Dickie Lonning

Todcroft

Sch

Weirs

162

PO

Pikes

209

Upton

Cat Crags

GET LOST
37

Keep an eye out for the ruined farmhouse.

The last stile is made of slate.

page 169). Head north-east over the field, through a gate and then to a sheepfold in the top corner of the next field. Go over the stile on the other side of the sheepfold. Your next key point to reassure you that you are on the right path are the ruins of a former farm. Keep to the left of these and head into the northern corner and through a gate. This will take you towards Brownrigg Hall Farm. Keep the drystone wall on your left and you'll eventually see a modern slate stile over the wall and onto the open gorse. Stick by the wall until you reach the farm track and follow this a few yards north until you double back on the single-track road leading past Knocker House. It drops

GET LOST

38

down into the village and brings you back to the car park. (Alternatively, coming from Brownrigg proceed around the top of the wall – rough but OK – to join the old road down to Caldbeck past Knocker House.)

ESKDALE

IT'S always good to have an excuse for returning to the lovely Lake District valley of Eskdale so it was a delight to discover a Postman's Path in this beautiful part of the world. It was recorded in *Walking in the Lake District* by HH Symonds, published in 1933, and seems to have been a short-cut for the postman between Gill Bank Farm beyond the village of Boot

GET LOST
39

and the Woolpack Inn at the top end of the Eskdale Valley. This would have been a convenient short cut past Eel Tarn to the Woolpack Inn, saving the postie a long walk or cycle ride back out of the village and along the valley road. This postman's trod is a short-ish walk (allow about one hour) which gives you dramatic views over the fells and valley. It also offers you a glimpse at the truly wild spot of Eel Tarn and we recommend resting there to enjoy the scenery and have your picnic. Or you may prefer to lunch at the Woolpack before returning on the main road along the valley bottom to the village of Boot.

GET LOST 40

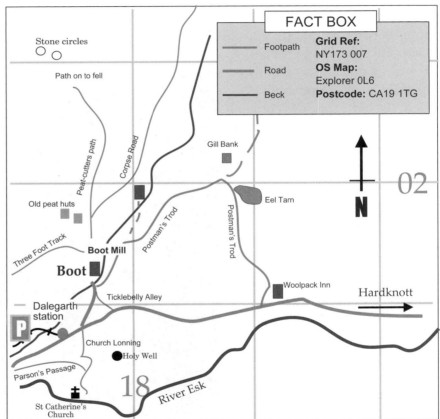

Stone circles

Path on to fell

Peat-cutters path

Corpse Road

Gill Bank

Old peat huts

Three Foot Track

Boot Mill

Boot

Postman's Trod

Postman's Trod

Eel Tarn

Woolpack Inn

Hardknott

Ticklebelly Alley

Dalegarth station

Church Lonning

Holy Well

Parson's Passage

River Esk

St Catherine's Church

FACT BOX

——	Footpath	**Grid Ref:** NY173 007
——	Road	**OS Map:** Explorer 0L6
——	Beck	**Postcode:** CA19 1TG

02

N

18

POSTMAN'S TROD: BOOT MILL TO THE WOOLPACK

THIS postman's path is a fairly tough but exhilarating walk from Boot to the Woolpack Inn. Pubs at either end make it a pleasant one too. Walk to the end of the village of Boot. We recommend calling in to see Boot Mill but our path turns right before the bridge and wends its way up the hill with Whillan Beck on your left. The steep climb up onto the fell is made easier by the well-made lane and the wonderful views back over Boot. You don't go as far as Gill Bank but turn right onto the fell through a gate. You will follow the signpost pointing to Eel Tarn, not the one to

The postbox near the Woolpack Inn, Eskdale.

'Woolpack'. Then continue up hill with the fell wall on your left and follow the clear track

onto the fell. Eel Tarn will eventually be on your right but it is a natural dip/amphitheatre so you won't see the tarn until you are right on top of it. It's a good spot to have your bait.

You then walk around the western edge of the tarn and drop down into the valley. You will pass a derelict stone-built hut. The path comes off the fell and through a gate between houses before rejoining the main road. Appropriately there is a postbox at the end of the path. Turn left for the Woolpack or turn right to take the main road back to Boot.

GET LOST

41

The Lickle Valley

GET
LOST
42

POSTMAN'S TROD AT LICKLE VALLEY

WE are grateful to blogger Martha Love (marthalovesblog.blogspot.com) for details of this postman's route which runs between the Lickle Valley and Duddon Valley. Her parents moved to the area in the 1970s and she grew up with tales of the postman in living memory cycling from one valley to the other. Its purpose, clearly as with the other postman's trods, was to save the postie time cycling out of one valley and back into the other. Once you have climbed onto the terraced path you will find it an easy, well-made route. We suggest a circular route around Raven's Crag and Brown Haw to make this a satisfying two-hour walk.

START: Stephenson Ground – but park at Broughton Moor car park at SD248924 (post code LA20 6AH). There are not many parking places in this part of the world so we're suggesting a 'start' point at an official car park. It's a short walk away from the true beginning of the postman's trod which means you will have a safe place to park – and a nice warm-up before the proper start to your walk. In fact there are a few small parking places in close proximity at this point on Broughton Moor so if one is full, hopefully there is a space at another one.

These 'dog-gates' beside stiles can be lifted up for your pet to go through and save you carrying your dog over the stile.

GET LOST

43

THE WALK: We suggest parking at the southern most end of the wood and starting from the footpath at that end. However, this is a wood with many paths and you can take any of them to the road leading to Stephenson Ground.

Drop down through the woods. A small beck runs through the bottom of the valley with the ruins of a former mill and charming bridge beside it. Climb up the other side and follow the path until you reach the road. You may wish to make a note (or better still take a photo) at various points so you can be sure of your correct path back. Turn

GET LOST

44

The bridge over Appletree Worth Beck en route to the Postman's Trod.

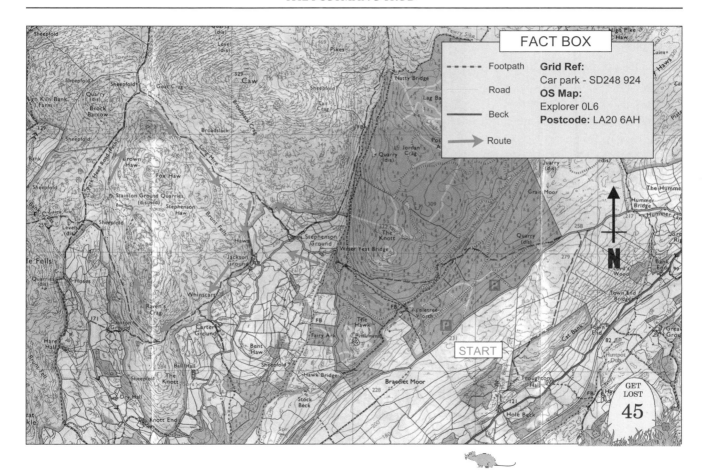

FACT BOX

- - - - Footpath
——— Road
——— Beck
——→ Route

Grid Ref:
Car park - SD248 924
OS Map:
Explorer 0L6
Postcode: LA20 6AH

START

GET LOST
45

right at the road and you'll follow this over Water Yeat Bridge. As the road climbs up hill you'll notice a curious drystone structure on your right. I'm happy to be corrected as to what this is but I am guessing it is the remains of a fox bield – a trap to catch foxes. You'll reach Stephenson Ground at the top of the hill and you go through the first gate on your right. There are footpath signs and you want the one heading north-west. It's a well-made path which eventually drops down into the valley. We will turn left at this point. The path is not clear but head for just above the barns of Jackson Ground and you'll pick up the

This curious construction is possibly an old fox bield.

path adjacent to a drystone wall. Once you reach the path across Carter Ground you will find it

an easier well-marked path that gives grand views across the fells. It's likely the postman having delivered the post at Stephenson Ground, Jackson Ground and Carter Ground dropped into Duddon Valley at Stainton Ground but we're going to carry on in a circular route so stay on the terrace path as it loops round, heading north. Anywhere along here is a good place to stop for your picnic.

When you reach the top of the valley, turn right onto the Park Head Road path. At the crest you'll be looking towards Seathwaite. The path is quite clear and once over the crest, turn right on to Long Mire. This takes you through the valley back to the start. The path fizzles out but you'll recognise your starting point and can happily return via Stephenson Ground and the wood to the car park.

PUBLIC TOILETS: None

REFRESHMENTS: There is the Blacksmiths Arms at LA20 6AX. Or head into the village of Broughton in Furness. We always go to the delightful Village Bakery but there are plenty of other fine cafes and pubs in the village.

Heading home: Along the Postman's Path in the Lickle Valley.

GET LOST
47

THE FAIRY POSTMAN

WHEN Sir Francis Radclyffe was made a peer in 1688 he used the name of Keswick's lake for his earldom. The Earls of Derwentwater were evidently well loved by the people of Keswick. The third Earl, James (Francis' grandson) would, however, lose the peerage in dramatic style: He was a prominent Jacobite and in 1716 was convicted of high treason and executed at the Tower of London. Although his country seat was in Dilston in Northumberland, he had a home on an island on Derwentwater – which was therefore called

Looking out from Castle Crag towards Lord's Island.

Lord's Island. The great affection in which he was held by Keswickians is probably shown

through the legends that survive about him. It is said, for example, that on the night of his execution a particularly brilliant display of the northern lights occurred and they were henceforth called Lord Derwentwater's Lights. And it is said his wife, fleeing the island with the family treasure, scrambled up the side of Walla Crag (previously believed to be inaccessible) and it is now known as Lady's Rake. Some gold coins she supposedly dropped have, legend says, been found on the route. But it is worth mentioning that another legend says she threw the treasure into Derwentwater.

The legend of a fairy postman

who visited the Earl of Derwentwater is noted in 1903 by author Thomas Carrick. In his book, *The Border Land*, he talks about the belief in fairies along the Borders (between England and Scotland). He says: "They were neither wholly human, nor divine, nor demoniacal, but a kind of medley of all three – a strange mixture of body and spirit – and they could assume either, or both, as the case demanded or necessity arose. They were called by particular names, according to the place

GET
LOST
49

The Fairy Postman stone at Fourstones, Northumberland. Grid Ref: NY895 678.

where they dwelt, the work they did, or the aspect they assumed."

In telling of the fairy postman he says: "When the last Earl of Derwentwater was undecided as to whether or not he should join the standard of the rebellion, he was alone on the banks of the river, in great distress of mind, cogitating what to do. As he was leaning against a tree, a phantom-like person delivered to him a letter, and mysteriously vanished. That letter decided him, and sealed his doom. That visitant is called the Fairy Postman to this day."

GET LOST
50

CARLISLE'S LINK WITH POSTAL HISTORY

A replica 'Penfold' pillar box can be found in Carlisle city centre. It commemorates the first post box in mainland Britain being erected in nearby Botchergate in 1853 (one already existed on the Channel Islands). The Botchergate one no longer survives but there is a plaque at the site.

This is, unusually, one legend where we might be able to ascertain the origins. In 1863 Sarah Smith-Jones wrote a history of the Earls of Derwentwater and she includes this note:

"There is a fanciful tradition left in the neighbourhood of Dilston which from the romance attaching to it will very likely long remain but which we can scarce deem worthy of any reliance. In this it is stated that Lord Derwentwater maintained a correspondence with his friends at this time by means of letters deposited in a hollow stone called by the people generally the fairy stone but which was in truth an old Roman altar situated a little to the west of Hexham. These letters the tradition affirms to have been brought and deposited by a little boy very beautifully dressed in green the fairy colour while such was the superstition of the people at that period that although he was seen and noticed frequently they dared on no account intermeddle with his doings as being a messenger from fairy land. Those who were in pursuit of the Earl would not be very likely to be long withheld by such scruples however neither would intelligence so deposited be safe so there is little likelihood that either the Earl or his friends would trust it there."

But it would be a shame to lose such a delightful legend so quickly. Just imagine a tree in Keswick where, when you are unable to make a difficult decision, the fairy postman – a little boy beautifully dressed in green – brings you a letter which makes the decision for you. Even if, as in the case of the third Earl, it's most definitely the wrong one!

Credit is due to Andy Curtis for his research on this legend – see heddonhistory.weebly.com/blog/fairy-tale

Postman Pat bridge at Longsleddale

In the footsteps of Postman Pat

THE children's character Postman Pat with his black and white cat Jess was created by John Cunliffe and his inspiration came from his local post office in Kendal. Sadly, 'Mrs Groggins' post office' closed in 2003 but you can still post a letter in the post box outside the cottage. It's just a short walk out of Kendal town centre on Beast Banks and there is a Postman Pat collection box outside and a plaque on the wall (see picture right). But if you're looking for a day out we're going to suggest a trip into the valley of Longsleddale which was the inspiration for Greendale, the valley where

"The Greendale roads seemed more twisty and twiny than ever. Sometimes Pat wished he could fly like a bird and pop the letters and parcels down people's chimneys, like Father Christmas!"

Postman Pat delivered his letters and had his adventures. The packhorse bridge at Sadgill at the end of the valley was used at the start of the TV programmes with Postman Pat seen driving over it. Time it right and you can still see a red postvan driving over it to the farm! Longsleddale has one road. It's a narrow single-track road and it's easy to

imagine as you drive along it that you are Postman Pat on one of his adventures. But such a long single-track road can get tedious so we have a couple of suggestions to make it easier for you. First, consider hiring bikes and cycling into the valley. It's a short ride north out of Kendal on the A6 and then turn left into Longsleddale at Garnett Bridge. Alternatively we suggest driving into the valley as far as the church (about halfway along the valley). There is parking opposite the church (and a public toilet). Postcode is LA8 9BB and Grid reference is NY500 028. You can then enjoy a leisurely walk to Sadgill.

GET LOST
54

St Mary's Church at Longsleddale, complete with postbox. There is parking opposite and a public toilet.

A Hero Postman

WE cannot leave this homage to postmen (and women) without doffing our postman's cap to one of the county's unsung heroes: William Brockbank of Ulverston (although another source says he lived at Millom). He walked more than 50 miles a day, six days a week delivering letters and small parcels between Ulverston and Whitehaven. His accomplishments won him national publicity and he was dubbed 'the walking post'. He took up his job on July 5th 1798 and here's his route:

Ulverston to Broughton, 10 miles; Broughton to Bootle, 8 (a

'It is estimated he travelled 3,950 miles over his 79 days of working'

newspaper report notes "the road in this distance is very rough and bad, intersecting mountains, and many steep hills"). From Bootle to Ravenglass, 6; Ravenglass to Holmrook (this included wading through the river at Muncaster), 2; Holmrook to Calder Bridge, 2; Calder Bridge to Egremont, 4; Egremont to Whitehaven, 5. From Whitehaven he returned by the same route.

It was also noted that "upon his return to Ulverston, he delivered the letters through that town, and frequently went with letters to the distance of three or four miles from Ulverston, and on some occasions to Backbarrow, a distance of nine miles from Ulverston". He worked every day except Sunday. He was made redundant on October 4th that year when a mail coach was begun on the same route. It is estimated he travelled 3,950 miles over his 79 days of working. He moved to Glossop in Derbyshire in search of work where he again took up as a postman but walking a more leisurely 16 miles a day.

GET LOST

55

MORE POSTAL TRIVIA

CUMBRIA can be proud of a number of links with the postal service (not least William Wordsworth who was Distributor of Stamps for Westmorland from 1813 to 1843 – look out for the plaque in Church Street, Ambleside). His fellow poet Samuel Taylor Coleridge can perhaps claim credit for introducing the humble stamp following an incident that occurred at the start of the 19th Century while Coleridge was living at Greta Hall, Keswick. Before the Penny Black in 1840, the cost of postage was paid by the recipient. This led to much

skulduggery to avoid payment: the letter might be incorrectly addressed, have a coded mark on it, or perhaps an additional middle name of the recipient. These all allowed the recipient to receive a coded message from the sender. He or she would then have no need to obtain the letter and could decline to pay the postage. Coleridge told the following tale and it was used by the father of the postage stamp, Rowland Hill, to argue for postal reform:

"One day, when I had not a shilling which I could spare, I was passing by a cottage not far from Keswick, where a letter-carrier was demanding a shilling for a letter, which the woman of

the house appeared unwilling to pay, and at last declined to take. I paid the postage, and when the man was out of sight, she told me that the letter was from her son, who took that means of letting her know that he was well; the letter was not to be paid for. It was then opened and found to be blank!"

There are other Postman's Paths around Britain including one at Rhenigidale on the Isle of Harris (2rhenigidale.co.uk/deal/ the-postmans-path) and on the Shetland Islands (www.heritagepaths.co.uk/path details.php?path=143)

Right: Mackenzie's Lonning, Cleator Moor.

GET LOST
56

Down't lonnings

GET
LOST
57

Cumbria's lonnings

"Ther' cannot be annuder spot so private an' so sweet,
As Billy Watson' lonnin' of a lownd summer neeght!"

— Billy Watson' Lonnin' – Alexander Craig Gibson

LONNING is simply a dialect term for a lane but it is a specific type of lane. Lonnings are usually low-level, about half a mile long and often end at a farm. The latter characteristic probably explains the origin of the term. 'Loan' was a word for 'the quiet place by the farm' and was where villagers would buy eggs or other produce; hence the path to the loan became the lonning. In the north-east the term is spelt 'lonnen' and refers more to a narrow street than a country path. While all lanes in Cumbria can rightly be called lonnings there are a number that have quite specific names: Johnnie Bulldog Lonning, Gipsy Lonning, Tatie Pot Lonning, Lovely Lonning, Dynamite Lonning, Fat Lonning, Thin Lonning and even Squeezy Gut Lonning. You won't usually find these names on any map. The local villagers know them and can point out where they are but they hide themselves from Ordnance Survey, Google or Bing. The good news is that most are public footpaths and present an opportunity for a

GET LOST
58

short, pleasant walk. As they are low-level, short and generally traffic-free they make an ideal ramble for the whole family. Although they rarely exist on maps, we have chosen a few of our favourites and detailed where they are. They are all marked as public footpaths on the Ordnance Survey map and can be found on our Bing map at https://binged.it/2JvHBJe. Remember you can change the

Billy Watson's Lonning at Harrington is the subject of a famous dialect ballad written 200 years ago by Alexander Craig Gibson. The ballad says of all the lonnings in the district, there's none as private and so sweet as Billy Watson's Lonning on a 'lownd summer neeght'. Lownd means 'still, quiet'.

GET
LOST
59

Bing map view to one showing Ordnance Survey maps which will help you locate the path.

SEACROSS LONNING

BUT we will start with two that are named on the OS map: Seacross Lonning and Green Lonning near Wythop Mill. We're not sure why these lonnings have been so honoured but they make a good circular walking route that lasts about an hour. Wythop Mill is a charming hamlet to the west of Keswick but there is no easy parking there so we recommend driving a bit further west to the church of St

Seacross Lonning is also known as *Boggle* Lonning as locals believed it haunted by the ghost of a man who once hanged himself in the lonning. Opposite page: Author Alan Cleaver in Seacross Lonning.

Cuthbert's. You'll find easier parking here and if you time it right, you will arrive the same day as the church is holding one of its famous cream tea afternoons! Walk about a quarter of a mile east from the church and you'll find Seacross Lonning on your left. It's the first footpath you come to on your left and is signposted. Drop down the slope and turn right into the lonning proper. The first part of the lonning is encased in hazel and makes for a cool walk in the summer. We've seen red squirrels here so keep an eye open. At the end of the lonning there is a bridge over the beck and you walk out into Wythop Mill. Turn right and head uphill

GET
LOST
61

before turning right again on the road back to the church. You can, however divert up Green Lonning which you'll find on your left just as you leave Wythop Mill. It's a gradual slope up and then opens out to offer splendid views over the valley below. Green Lonning is about half a mile long and you then turn right and head back to the church through Beckhouse.

You'll also note on the map that there is a corpse road nearby. This would have once led to Lorton church but now fizzles out at the top of Ling Fell; no matter, it still makes for a good walk with great views.

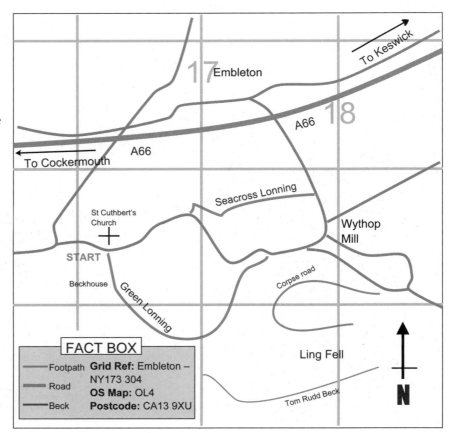

FACT BOX

Footpath
Road
Beck

Grid Ref: Embleton –
NY173 304
OS Map: OL4
Postcode: CA13 9XU

GET LOST

62

LOW LONNING

THE charming village of Gosforth in the west of the county is home to the beautiful Low Lonning and is also a jumping-off point for Wasdale, Eskdale and other locations in West Cumbria. There is easy parking in the village. Low Lonning is sandwiched between the road to Wasdale and the road to Eskdale but it's clear that at one time this was the main route in and out of Wasdale, with a suggestion that it continued to the coast at Seascale, even being used by smugglers. Certainly documents easily date it back 200 years (it is also on the first edition OS map published in 1865) and the

Gosforth: The West Cumbrian village is a good starting point for a number of intriguing walks.

impressive stone bridge that crosses the River Bleng in the lonning tells of a time when this lonning was used by heavy traffic. For much of its route the lonning is sheltered but occasionally you catch a glimpse into the Wasdale Valley.

PARKING: Either park in the village (there is a car park with an honesty box for a donation); it is then a one-mile walk to the start of the lonning on the Eskdale road. Or park considerately on the main road into Wasdale. There is only space for one car at the start of the lonning on the Eskdale road.

GET
LOST
63

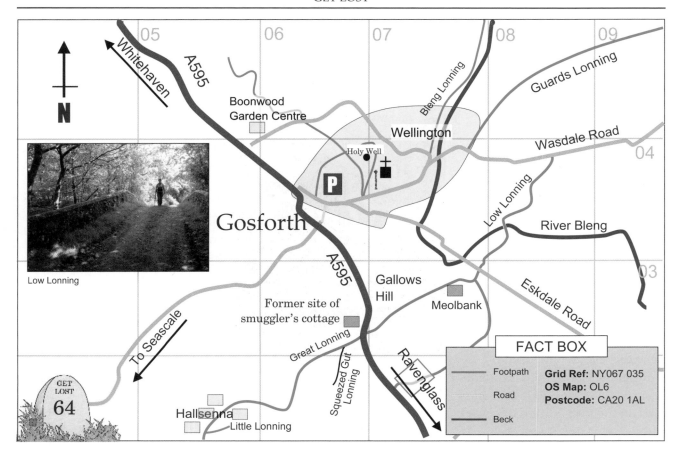

N

Whitehaven

A595

05 06 07 08 09

Boonwood
Garden Centre

Bleng Lonning

Guards Lonning

Wellington

Wasdale Road

Holy Well

04

P

Low Lonning

Low Lonning

Gosforth

River Bleng

A595

03

Gallows
Hill

Meolbank

Eskdale Road

To Seascale

Former site of
smuggler's cottage

Great Lonning

Ravenglass

GET
LOST
64

Squeezed Gut
Lonning

Hallsenna

Little Lonning

FACT BOX

Footpath

Road

Beck

Grid Ref: NY067 035
OS Map: OL6
Postcode: CA20 1AL

DISTANCE: 415 metres. It is a relatively flat and easy walk; much of it is a well-made track but it can get muddy. Horses use Low Lonning so keep dogs and children under control.

START: NY094 040. You can walk this lonning either way of course but parking is easier on the Wasdale (north) side. Walk down the main track, bearing to the right. You will walk past some houses (Rainors) – don't worry it's a public footpath – and be afforded some glorious views of Wasdale and its famous *screes*. Halfway along the lonning you will reach the bridge over the River Bleng – the perfect spot for your *bait*. Continue along the lonning until you reach the Eskdale road. You

GET LOST

65

can then turn right and walk back into Gosforth or return along the lonning to your car on the Wasdale road.

EXPLORING FURTHER

IF you wish to extend your walk you can cross the road and continue on the path heading south-west towards the coast. You'll walk through Meolbank and the path then rises up onto Gallows Hill (sometimes Gallus-Hill – gallus is an old English word for gallows). The actual Gallows Hill is on the north side of the footpath. Legend says criminals were hanged at this

Looking from Gallows Hill with the Western Fells in the background.

spot. We can't be sure of that but if you're going to leave this world in a hurry, you might as well have had a fantastic view of the fells for your last sight of the world. The path continues to a caravan park and the busy A595 (take care if you cross the road). Over the road is a single track to the hamlet of Hallsenna. This track was known as Great Lonning and it will take you on to the coast. A short way down there is a 'pull-in' for cars and this was the start of Squeezed Gut Lonning – always a narrow path but a farmer told us that many years ago she drove cattle down there. Today it is impossible to access and is more of a wide hedge than a path. But in Hallsenna itself you will find

GET LOST
66

another lonning: Little Lonning. This fizzles out but it's worth taking a peek. You can continue on the track past various farms until you reach Seascale and the coast.

SMUGGLING

AUTHOR Graham Sutton investigated Hallsenna's links with smuggling for his 1948 book, *Fell Days* and spoke to a farmer near Hallsenna about a cottage called Benfold or Mary Largs that stood near the start of

Little Lonning can be found at the end of Great Lonning which passes through the hamlet of Hallsenna.

GET LOST 67

Great Lonning (eastern end). He wrote:

It's now impossible to walk down Squeezed Gut Lonning but this is the external view.

"The place was called Marylands. It was pulled down 'a while back' and rebuilt somewhere else. The 'smuggler's whoal' had been a vault, concealed till recently by the flagged floor of the house which fell in, and a foal with it. So the farmer had it filled up. But before doing so he removed the flags (dressed stone being precious) and discovered what-like the hole was: stone-floored, stone-sided, seven foot square and eight deep, with no way into it that he could see unless you'd shifted a flag; the old lads had stored cargoes there, like enough. He told me too that the last tenant, a woman, was hanged for smuggling on a gallows-hill in the neighbourhood; which hints that the while-back of which he spoke was remote."

Nothing remains of the cottage Marylands but spare a thought for the woman who was hanged for smuggling when you walk down Gallows Hill.

EXPLORING GOSFORTH

GOSFORTH itself is a charming village with tearooms and pubs, gift shops, a village hall, a volunteer-run library and a real community

Gosforth holy well: The site itself is in a rather poor state but it's worth a visit for the views across the landscape.

spirit. The church is famed for its Gosforth Cross (pictured left), an impossibly thin and tall cross which has survived since the 10th Century AD and a short walk above the church is the neglected St Mary's holy well. The village is the perfect spot for a bite to eat or drink before setting off on your walk – and again on your return. It is worth visiting Gosforth Church, not least to see Gosforth Cross which stands in the churchyard. It dates from the first half of the tenth century and has a curious mix of Norse Pagan and Christian imagery on it, including the apocalypse. Inside the church you will also find two carved Viking hogback stones and other historic artefacts. Just a short walk from the church is St Mary's Well (NY 073 041). This is in a poor condition (at one time there was a chapel over it) but it's worth visiting as you are rewarded with views over the surrounding countryside. You can continue up the hill then turn left (south-west) and return to the village via Blennerhazel.

GET LOST

69

ALSO NEARBY

THERE are a couple more lonnings nearby including Guards Lonning which is the first footpath on the left as you climb out of Wellington on the Wasdale road. It is a mile and a half long, taking you into the Wasdale valley. A shorter walk is the Long Walk at Calder Bridge (just to the north of Gosforth). It follows the River Calder east from the church to the (private) ruins of Calder Abbey.

Long Walk beside the River Calder and Calder Abbey.

LOVERS LONNING

THERE are a number of Lovers Lonnings – those quiet lanes where one might take your beau on a romantic walk. Billy Watson's Lonning quoted at the start of this chapter was one such lane. One that has the name Lovers Lonning can be found at St Bees (Grid Ref: NX977 101) – though it appears to have moved over the years! It is now listed as dropping down from the B5345 south of St Bees onto the Coulderton Road and it is a charming and romantic walk offering views over the Irish Sea towards the Isle of Man. You can park in a lay-by on the B5345 and drop down Lovers Lonning. If you then turn right on the

The coffin rest on the St Bees to Coulderton Road. A coffin rest was a place where mourners paused on their route to the church to sing a hymn or say a prayer. Grid Ref: NX974 103.

road you will pass a coffin rest at the side of the road. This is on the Coulderton to St Bees corpse road (such paths were used to take the dead from remote parishes to the 'mother' church) and shortly after you turn left down another path to the shore. Historical records show it was this path that was originally 'Lovers Lonning' but today it is in a poor state of repair. The corpse road would likely have followed this path and then followed the beck to the Priory.

St Bees is the 'seaside' capital of West Cumbria offering sandy beaches for the family and a village boasting a number of pubs to get a

GET LOST

71

drink or meal. You can also take a walk on to St Bees Head to enjoy the views out to sea or look at the birds nesting there (you will find an RSPB reserve on the Head).

St Bees is the start of the Coast 2 Coast walk which was devised by Alfred Wainwright. It ends 182 miles later at Robin Hood's Bay in Yorkshire. The start of the walk takes you over St Bees Head and via Sandwith before heading east and through the Lake District. With respect to Wainwright this is not the most logical or prettiest of starts to the walk so we detail here our own

Pictured on previous page: Lovers Lonning at St Bees and (inset) the entrance to the original Lovers Lonning.

version which takes you through some of the oldest paths in St Bees before re-joining Wainwright's C2C at Cleator.

AN ALTERNATIVE COAST 2 COAST START

OUR start to the C2C begins on a Pitman's Trod (pictured right) that heads out of St Bees skirting the northern boundary of Fleatham House hotel. This was the route used by miners to walk from the village to the mines at Pallaflat and Bigrigg. These were iron ore mines (although coal mining was also a major industry in West Cumbria until the 1980s)

Stepping out on the Pitman's Trod past Fleatham House, St Bees.

GET LOST
73

and they were worked for the most part until 1914. Poor signposting means the start of the trod can be hard to find. Head east down Finkle Street past the Fleatham House hotel. Turn into Fleatham Croft and the path starts at the end of that cul-de-sac. The trod takes you up hill to Loughrigg Farm and you can then follow a minor road to the hamlet of Pallaflat. Continue on to Bigrigg. Turn left on the A595 past the garage and turn right into Springfield Gardens (beside the Old Captain's House pub). At the end you join another pit path that takes you on to Cleator. You will cross a disused railway which now forms part of the Sustrans cycle

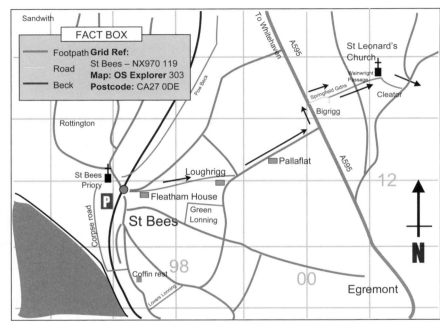

FACT BOX

	Grid Ref:
Footpath	St Bees – NX970 119
Road	Map: OS Explorer 303
Beck	Postcode: CA27 0DE

network. Then turn right onto a single track path that puts you back on the official C2C route. This is actually a former corpse road that leads you to St Leonard's Church at Cleator and you will also pass through Wainwright's Passage shortly before the church. This is named after Alfred Wainwright.

GET LOST

74

Mackenzie's Lonning

CLEATOR Moor was ravaged by industry in the 19th Century as mines were dug and railways built to extract the valuable minerals. But the legacy are some extensive stretches of cycle paths where the railways used to be. Mackenzie's Lonning is close to the town centre and a short drop down from the Sustrans cycle path. For part of the way it is a 'sunken' lane. Grid Ref: NY014 143.

Mackenzie's Lonning, Cleator Moor which is off the Sustrans cycle track leading to Jacktrees Road.

GET LOST
75

CYCLE PATHS

IF you and your family love cycling then it is worth checking out the Sustrans cycle paths that exist in West Cumbria (see sustrans.org.uk). These largely follow the former railway lines used in the past by the mining industry. You will still see remnants of the mining past beside the cycle paths. In West Cumbria, routes 71 and 72 are mostly traffic-free and stretch from Workington to Egremont.

GET LOST
76

Pictured right is the Sustrans cycle path at Cleator Moor.

OTHER LONNINGS

WE have collected nearly 200 named lonnings in Cumbria and you'll find them detailed on our map at http://tiny.cc/37hm9y. Here are just some you may wish to visit.

Thin and Fat Lonnings, Maryport (NY043 370): Park beside Netherhall School. You will see Thin Lonning and Fat Lonning across the road (pictured). Thin Lonning's actual name is Pigeonwell Lonning but its nickname arises from the adjacent 'fat' lonning. Start walking up Fat Lonning on the right. This will drop you down to the golf course and you can turn left to walk the coastal path as far as the Senhouse Museum.

The entrances to Thin and Fat Lonnings.

The museum is well worth a visit of course. Many of the Roman artefacts on display come from the nearby Roman fort. Return to your car via Thin Lonning; you will soon discover why it is called 'Thin'. There's room for one person only at most parts!

The 'bridge' on Thin Lonning.

GET LOST

77

Huntingstile Lonning, Grasmere (NY334 062): This lonning is the subject of a famous ballad read most years at the Grasmere Christmas Readings. *Down't Lonnin* sets the Christmas story in Huntingstile. The lonning (pictured right) is also part of the corpse road from Chapel Stile to Grasmere – a relatively easy 90-minute walk with cafes and pubs at both ends. The lonning gradually rises up from the lakeside road on to the fell. We have observed red squirrels here and even on one occasion an otter! It is beautiful at all times of the year but particularly autumn.

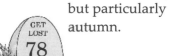

GET LOST

78

Johnnie Bulldog Lonning, Carlisle (NY427 562): If you are visiting Carlisle you may wish to pop along to Tesco near Junction 43 of the M6 for a surprisingly sweet lonning just beside the superstore. The lonning is named after Johnnie MacElroy who lived in the lonning at the end of the 19th Century. And he had a bulldog. It's a short walk down here to the river where you can enjoy a picnic.

Tatie Pot Lonning, Burgh by Sands (NY320 591): The parish council website details some delightful walks on its website (burghbysandsparishhall.co.uk) including this lonning which once housed a bakery making the Cumbrian 'delicacy' of Tatie Pot. It's also worth exploring the *kests* in the lanes nearby.

Wine Lonning, Kirkbride (NY228 574): You will find this charming but short lonning opposite the church. It was apparently used as a smugglers' route down to the Solway estuary.

GET LOST
79

**Gipsy Lonning,
Little Orton (NY358 547):** One of the few lonnings to have earned the honour of having its name on a signpost. Though it's also known as Farmers Lonning. There is a ghost of a six-foot tall cloaked figure who haunts this lonning. It is however a peaceful walk away from the noise of Carlisle.

**Whinnah Lonning,
Lamplugh (NY079 205):** This is surely one of the county's more ancient lonnings. Park in the lay-by off the A5086 at Millgillhead. In the past the lonning would have gone through the farm but now there is a short diversion around it. The village's funeral hearse was once kept at the eastern end of the lonning. You may also wish to view the nearby coffin rest at NY080 207.

**Miry Lonning,
Cumwhinton (NY448 517):** Miry is a dialect word for 'boggy' or 'swampy'. There may indeed be miry parts of this lonning if it's been raining hard but generally it's an easy and family-friendly walk near the village of Cumwhinton. Nearby is the less satisfying **Dog Lonning** (NY452 525) which presumably gets its name from the dog-leg in the path.

Back Lane

"There are walkers about today who do not seem to be aware that the true joys of the fells are to be found only by travelling leisurely"

— Alfred Wainwright

THE James Cropper Paper Mill at Burneside near Kendal has been providing employment to the local community since 1845. Its high quality papers are used all over the world, not least for the Royal British Legion's paper poppies each year. James Robinson started work there in the mid-19th Century and as he lived in the neighbouring village of Bowston he walked to and from work each day along Back

'By dint of frequent perambulation, at all times of the year and at all hours of the day, I have become familiar with the natural garniture of the lane'

— James Robinson, 1878

Lane until his retirement in 1881. He was also a nature writer and poet so took the opportunity to observe and record the flora and fauna along the lane. These notes he published in *A Country Lane: Its Flora and Fauna* in 1878 and they demonstrate his knowledge of nature and a talent for sharing his love of the trees, flowers and animals that became his constant companions to and from work. The lane still exists

GET LOST
81

though it is now a single-track tarmacked lane and the 'high hedges which afford a winter's shelter and a summer's shade' are these days trimmed a lot tighter than Mr Robinson may have liked. But it's a pleasant walk and you can return by a path that runs beside the river for a chance to glimpse an even wider range of wildlife. Mr Robinson's book ran to just 28 pages but is crammed full with details of over 50 plants and nearly 30 birds and animals. Sadly, it is long out of print but you can find a free digital version on archive.org and buy print-on-demand versions. It was also reprinted and wonderfully

annotated by Sue Shiels in 2013 in *A Country Lane Revisited* which brought the book and its lane to our attention. Sue and the Burneside Heritage Group compared the lane and its biodiversity in 1878 with how it fared in 2013.

Back Lane and, inset, Robinson's original book.

GET LOST 82

GET
LOST
83

THAT very handsome bird the Chaffinch or Spink, with its cheery 'tweet, tweet,' or 'pink, pink' enlivens the lane during the spring and summer. A pair build their nest in the forked branch of a crooked Crab Tree. It is a model of neatness and beauty, and so skilfully placed and made, in its exterior, so like the bark of the tree itself, that even the piercing eyes of a prowling school-boy would have some difficulty in detecting it. It generally contains four or five eggs of a dullish blue, or green, with a slight admixture of red. The nest of the Dunnock, (which, though very compact, is not to be compared in architectural beauty or skilful concealment with that of the Spink) is still

An excerpt from *The Country Lane* by James Robinson

lower, in the thick of the hedge; while that of the Redbreast is cleverly concealed in the grassy bank. The plaintive Yellow-hammer utters his 'chit, chit churr' during the spring, and no doubt builds somewhere in the vicinity.

Amongst the occasional visitors to the lane must be mentioned the Blue Tit, with its brilliant plumage; the Cole Tit; the Tom Tit; and the pretty Long-tailed Tit the last of which comes in flocks of about a dozen (probably a family),

and restlessly flits from tree to tree. The Whitethroats arrive late in the spring, and leave again during the summer. The

Redbreast and the Wren appear to remain in the lane all the year through. I have seen them there very early in the morning, and late in the evening, and suspect that of all small birds they are the first to rise and the last to retire. A bold and valorous bird is the Wren. To some of his deeds of daring I have been a witness. Often is he seen perched on the highest twig in the hedge, with bill extended to the utmost, pouring out his shrill treble. That such a volume of sound should proceed from such a tiny object is wonderful. Undisturbed by noisy traffic or juvenile foes the birds in my lane are comparatively tame, and apparently take little heed of my presence. One feathered visitor, however, seems to have a decided objection to my intrusion.

Back Lane near Burneside.

The crested lapwings, which in spring and summer take possession of the fields, on each side, continually cross and recross the road, and utter unceasingly their querulous 'peewits'."

GET LOST
85

THE WALK: Back Lane is close to Burneside, a village just north of Kendal off the A591 (Grid Ref: SD505 963). It's best to park in the village and walk past the famous James Cropper Paper Mill to Back Lane. The lane itself is an easy half-hour walk on a single-track road. Be aware of traffic using the road. It goes through to Bowston where James Robinson used to live and we recommend you return by the path beside the River Kent. Why don't you and members of your family copy James Robinson by writing a diary or blog detailing your walk and spotting as many flowers or birds as you can?

GET LOST

86

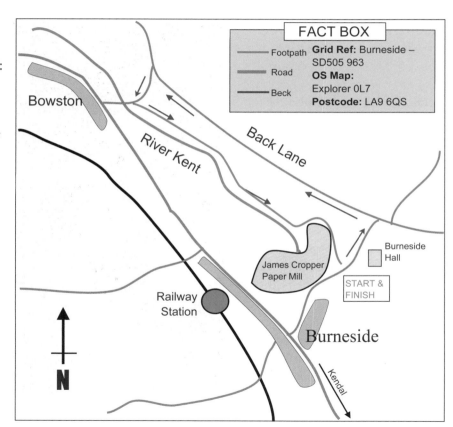

FACT BOX

—— Footpath
—— Road
—— Beck

Grid Ref: Burneside – SD505 963
OS Map: Explorer 0L7
Postcode: LA9 6QS

Bowston

River Kent

Back Lane

James Cropper Paper Mill

Burneside Hall

START & FINISH

Railway Station

Burneside

Kendal

N

Corpse roads

"Hark, hark. Death knocks"

Entry scribbled in the pages of the parish registers of Barton, Westmorland in 1776

THROUGHOUT Cumbria you will find the routes of the county's ancient corpse roads. These paths were used in medieval times to carry the dead from remote parishes to the 'mother' church and could sometimes stretch several miles. The mother churches made good money from funerals and were reluctant to relinquish their monopoly but by the late 18th Century most parishes had

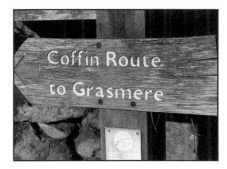

successfully petitioned the Bishop and been granted burial rights for their own churchyards. Fortunately for today's walkers, many corpse roads have survived as public footpaths. This is largely because it was a strong belief (though found erroneous when tested in the courts in 1899) that once you carried a body over a field that path became 'forever and a day' a public footpath. On occasion this belief led to farmers refusing

GET LOST 87

permission for mourners to take the dead over their land but it was generally overcome by a wonderful piece of rural logic: the family would rent the field off the farmer for the afternoon for a penny or a pin – a token gesture that ensured the farmer did not finish up with a public path over his land.

There are about 20 surviving corpse roads in Cumbria including famous ones at Rydal to Grasmere, Haweswater to Shap and Wasdale to Eskdale. Some are even fortunate to still have coffin rests in situ beside them. These wayside crosses or stones were points at which the

The coffin rest on the Rydal to Grasmere corpse road (close to Dove Cottage). Pictured right: The Sockbridge to Penrith corpse road at the Skirsgill end.

procession 'rested' while they sang a hymn or said prayers for the deceased. The final point on the procession was the lychgate at the entrance to the church.

There are sadly almost no contemporary records detailing the precise routes of most corpse roads so we have to rely on other local sources or oral tradition. These often came to the fore when there was a dispute over a particular footpath and villagers protested that the threatened path was an ancient corpse road so should be preserved. Such was the case at Irton in 1899 when Thomas Brocklebank closed off the footpath that ran past Irton Hall. Villagers took him to court and

produced a long line of witnesses and some centuries-old records that showed this had been the corpse road to St Paul's Church. A costly five-year legal battle eventually reached the High Court in London where it was ruled that the footpath should indeed remain open. The judge ruled that the villagers had shown the path had been regularly used as a public footpath for many years and should therefore remain public; this is the same 'test' used by government inspectors today when a right of way is disputed. The Irton corpse road still survives today, starting at Irton Hall, passing the legendary Irton

The Wasdale to Eskdale corpse road.

Oak and crossing fields to reach St Paul's Church. It is a short corpse road compared to many. The Wasdale to Eskdale corpse road is a tough five-mile walk over the fells, with the added hazard of the Burnmoor Tarn ghost. The legend tells how a man died and his corpse was tied to a horse to be carried over

GET LOST

90

the corpse road. But near the tarn the horse was startled and ran off into the mist. A long search failed to find horse or corpse. A few months later the man's mother died and her body was similarly tied to a horse to be taken over the corpse road to Eskdale. But the same thing happened again: the horse bolted and ran off into the mist. The search party did at last spot a horse and corpse by Burnmoor Tarn but when they reached it, they discovered it was the horse and body of the son; the mother was never found and it's said the mangled corpse of the horse and mother still haunt the corpse road.

You'll find a description of the routes of many of Cumbria's corpse roads in our book, *Corpse Roads of Cumbria*. We also devote several chapters to the traditions and superstitions surrounding death and funerals in the county. But here is one corpse road that is not too long, family-friendly and comes with the added advantage of being close to the Rheged Discovery Centre. This visitor attraction has cafes, shops, galleries, a huge cinema and plenty of activities for children. You'll find it just off the A66 west of Penrith. You can also park on the roads beside Greggs and Burger King closer to the M6 roundabout. As with so many corpse roads, we know about this one because of a legal dispute. In 1945 the path was being fought over and its status as a corpse road was used to

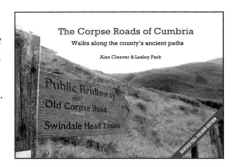

Find out more about corpse roads in our book, *The Corpse Roads of Cumbria*.

fight its corner. It began at the village of Sockbridge and led to St Andrew's church in the centre of Penrith. There was also mention of this corpse road going to and being used by the Lowther family on their nearby estate. It's more practical to do this corpse road in reverse but the M6 roundabout means the path now stops at Skirsgill. You'll also find near here a large ancient standing stone unceremoniously tucked away on the industrial estate. Also nearby but on private land is a holy well.

The standing stone on the industrial estate at Skirsgill.

THE WALK: To start this walk properly it's worth doubling back to Skirsgill. You may even wish to call and see the ancient standing stone. Follow the path through the gate and along a wooded lane to the railway tunnels. The path then drops gradually down towards the River Eamont. Cross the bridge and cut up through the field to Sockbridge. This is a residential village but you may wish to stay and enjoy a lunch at the Queen's Head Inn before making your return.

NEARBY: Visit Rheged Discovery Centre. You are also close to Penrith which has bookshops, cafes and pubs.

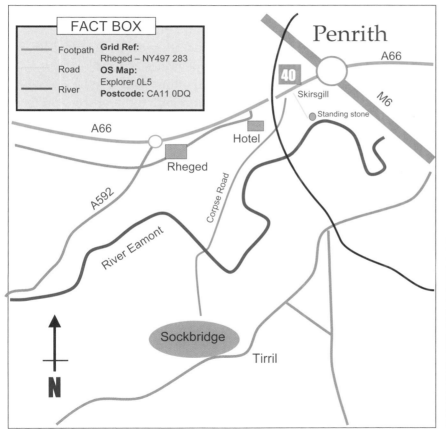

FACT BOX

～	Footpath	**Grid Ref:**
	Road	Rheged – NY497 283
	River	**OS Map:** Explorer 0L5
		Postcode: CA11 0DQ

Penrith

A66

40

Skirsgill

● Standing stone

M6

A66

Rheged

Hotel

A592

Corpse Road

River Eamont

Sockbridge

Tirril

N

The start of the corpse road at Skirsgill

GET LOST

93

OTHER CORPSE ROADS

Rydal to Grasmere: Start at Rydal Hall and follow the 'Coffin Route' signs. Grid Ref: NY365 063. Postcode: LA22 9LX.

Loweswater: Start at Loweswater Church and follow the path through Holme Wood to Fangs Brow. Grid Ref: NY134 210. Postcode: CA13 0RU

Shap: Pick up the path by Haweswater and follow the signs to Shap. This is a steep and long walk. Grid Ref: NY480 118. Postcode: CA10 2RP.

DEAD ENDS

PERHAPS surprisingly there are a few accounts of funeral processions getting lost on corpse roads. One occurred in the middle of the 18th Century on the corpse road from Lowside to Greystoke. It was the funeral of the Greystoke miller and he left £20 for food and drink for the villagers. But the mourners enjoyed this before the procession – and clearly enjoyed it well. They eventually set off for Greystoke in the early evening as fog began to descend, endeavouring to keep in a straight line. Despite their best efforts they took the wrong road and headed in the direction of Penrith. To quote an account of the event from 1893: "They had not gone far till they met old Squire Huddleston who, concluding from the unsteady appearance of the mourners, something was wrong, commanded the procession to stop, and inquired if the miller had desired his remains to be carried to market before burial. As may be imagined, there was great dismay among the leaders, each casting the blame on each other for the mistake."

When the procession eventually arrived at Greystoke church they forgot about the steps down from the porch and fell headlong, "the coffin fell on the top of them with a crash, bursting open the sides and revealing the shrouded body of the old miller."

Dobbies and Boggles

"As I was walking up the stair I met a man who wasn't there"

– Hughes Mearns

THE Harry Potter novels have popularised the rather obscure dialect term 'dobbie'. JK Rowling used the term for the Malfoy house elf but in its true Westmorland dialect form it had a wider meaning as a ghost, unexplained happening or anything odd. In neighbouring Cumberland (the two counties merged in 1974 to form Cumbria) the preferred term was boggle but the words meant the same; as one 19th

You biggots o' Worton, an other bit hamlets,
Be shamed o' yoursells, I think it full time;
For who wud have thowt to hear tell o' such doin's,
In the year eighteen hundred and forty and nine

– *Denham Tracts*

Century author wrote it was "anything expected to appear where they have no business to be". They may be a little scary but dobbies, boggles, ghosts or whatever you want to call them still hold a particular fascination and the county is fortunate to

have plenty of them. We've selected a couple of particularly scary stories with the consolation that they form part of a beautiful walk.

The Ealinghearth Dobbie deserves a special mention in the history of English ghosts: It is the only one as far as we can tell that has killed someone. It happened one dark and

GET LOST
95

stormy night (well, the 29th November 1849 if you want to be precise) when 16-year-old Christopher Cloudsdale – called 'Poor Kit' in the reports of his death – finished work at the bobbin mill at Finsthwaite where he was an apprentice. Thankfully, the mill still survives and is run today by English Heritage. He was sent on an errand to nearby Force Forge but instead of taking the most direct path through the woods decided instead to go across the fells. He told friends he was scared of encountering the Ealinghearth Dobbie

GET LOST
96

believed to haunt the woods so opted instead for the route over the

The death certificate of Christopher Cloudsdale. His inquest heard how a fear of meeting the Ealinghearth Dobbie had led to his death.

open fell. But a storm got up and when Kit did not return a search party was sent out. His body was eventually found on the fell where he had succumbed to the freezing cold conditions. As the *Westmorland Gazette* of 8th December 1849 rather colourfully described it...
"...the wandering of the boy could be traced in the woods adjacent to the road he ought to have taken, and on the moor by the balls of snow he had dashed from his clogs. To and fro the unfortunate lad had roamed amidst the 'pelting of that pitiless storm'. He must have been 'driven by the wind and battered by the

Pictured right: The path through the Rusland woods that 'Poor Kit' was too scared to walk

rain' and it is heart-rending to imagine the sufferings of that dreadful night to him."

The report concludes by saying: "Strange as it may appear, the unfortunate circumstance is attributed to a ghost story. In the highway between Rusland and Finsthwaite there is a place believed by the country folks to be haunted and sooner than go that way the poor lad had ventured over the hills on which he perished."

So who is this fearsome ghost? There are varying accounts but one tells of the suicide of a young woman at Rusland Pool (actually a beck, rather than a

Stott Park bobbin mill.

pool). The story recounted in a poem in 1900 tells of a young lady who lived at Ealinghearth Cottage. Her father was a man of ill temper who treated her badly. She falls in love and arranges to

meet her young man near Rusland Pool. Fearful of her plain looks she spends the housekeeping money her father gives her on a necklace being sold by a passing pedlar. When her father returns home he is furious that she has wasted the money on such a trinket. The girl runs out of the house in tears and drowns herself in Rusland Pool. The poem concludes by saying her father did not even attend her funeral saying he was too busy with his work to go. There are 19th Century tales of men in carts passing Rusland Pool stopping to offer a lift to a young sorrowful lady, only for the 'woman' to vanish as they approached Ealinghearth Cottage.

The Ghost of Ealinghearth by Mary Gregson was published in 1899. This is an extract…

Oh, I wonder – I wonder he came to love me;
For maids in the town are both fair and fine
In their costly gowns – he's so far above me
And I've only a flower to wear in mine!

"Only a flower? – and a bonny maiden,
Awaiting her lover who hastens nigh?
And with ribbons and trinkets my basket's laden"-
"Nay, pedlar, nay – but I dare not buy!
Nay, I've only the money my father lets me
For our household needs, and what would he say?"
"Nay, when he sees how this necklace sets thee
Where is the father could say thee nay?"

Only the necklace – he'll think her fairer -
The 'Somebody' coming from out the town
"It's not so much, and what could be rarer?"
And never a thought of her father's frown!
"Give ye good-e'en and a bright tomorrow"
And the pedlar laughs as he moves away
And her laugh rings back without thought of sorrow
When…. Her father stands in the way!

"And I toil all day and ye waste our living!"
And his face was set like the face of the dead -
Never a sign of love or forgiving,
Half-crazy with terror, she turned and fled
For anger's fire goes out in a minute,
And many harsh words ye may bear, and live;
But the anger with nought but coldness in it!
And ah, for the heart that will never forgive?

And there in the morning light they sought her,
Where the tide rolls inland, with strong, soft flow,
And bore her – the carrier's fair-haired daughter,
Up-banks to Ealinghearth, soft and slow
There is a snow-white shroud they arrayed her,
Laid rosemary-twigs on her maiden bier;
In Finsthwaite's churchyard they gently laid her
"You were weary, Sweetest – rest softly here!"

And her father followed, with face unaltered -
Till the sunbeams on Yewbarrow rested low
Then turned towards Ealinghearth – never faltered -
"Ye must bear her alone – I've my rounds to go!"

GET
LOST
99

BATTLE OF THE BEECHES

THE walk itself takes in the famous '99 Rusland beeches' – a popular beauty spot but one which rather incredibly the National Park were 'reluctantly' going to fell in 1996 because the trees were believed to be in a dangerous state. A rigorous public campaign saved the trees. The walk also includes a visit to the Stott Park Bobbin Mill where 'Poor Kit' once worked.

- Visit Rusland Horizons (www.ruslandhorizons.org) to find out more about the area.

GET LOST
100

Decision time: You can either take the long route along the main road to Rusland Cross or the shorter route on the permissive path to Yew Barrow.

THE WALK: A walk best done in autumn to see the '99 beeches' in all their beauty – but a pleasant walk any time of the year. We suggest parking at the public car park at Stott Park Bobbin Mill – the mill is of course well worth a visit. It is kept as a working mill by English Heritage so you can get a real flavour of where Poor Kit worked before his untimely death. Head uphill (south) away from the mill on the main road and you will pass through the beautiful village of Finsthwaite. Continue south along this road and after about a mile you reach a footpath sign directing you through a gate into the woods and Rusland's famous '99 beeches'. Keep an eye out for the

Ealinghearth dobbie as you wend your way through the wood and after about a mile you will reach Ellerside and the road to Rusland Cross. [You can take this road (north) for a longer walk: take the first right into Crosslands, then right again and the return path over the fell is a couple of hundred yards on your right beside a beck. It is a reasonably well sign-posted path but we would still recommend using a map and compass so you can take a bearing. It's a steep climb onto the top of the fell (where Poor Kit met his demise) and then it drops down into woodland, past High Dam and back to the car park.] A shorter route is taking the permissive path signposted

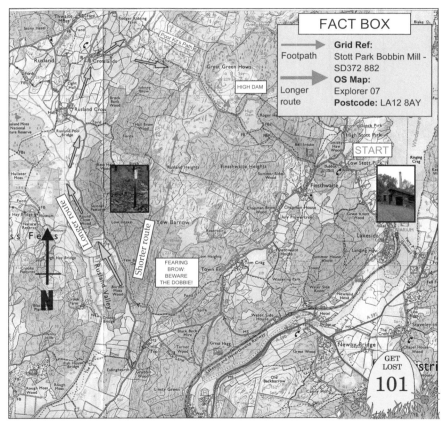

FACT BOX

Footpath

Longer route

Grid Ref:
Stott Park Bobbin Mill - SD372 882
OS Map:
Explorer 07
Postcode: LA12 8AY

START

HIGH DAM

Longer route

Shorter route

Rusland Valley

FEARING BROW BEWARE THE DOBBIE!

N

GET LOST

101

Yew Barrow which takes you north up through Yew Barrow Woods onto the fell. Interestingly, this area is known as Fearing Brow – fearing being an old word for an evil spirit. Be aware it is steep. There are white-tipped posts on the path to guide you and boards over the boggy parts. Once on the fell-top you can turn right (east) and drop down past High Dam to the car park. Both are reasonably tough routes so if you have less able walkers or children with you, you may prefer to take your *bait* in the woods at Ellerside and then return home the way you came.

High Dam makes for a perfect picnic spot on your return to Stott Park Bobbin Mill.

ALSO IN THE AREA: The vintage Lakeside and Haverthwaite Railway (LA12 8AL) runs from Haverthwaite to the southern end of Lake Windermere. The Lakeland Motor Museum is also nearby (LA12 8TA).

A S ghost stories go, this one is pretty gruesome! And you can still see the ruins where the murder allegedly took place. For an easy and short walk you can park in the car park in Miterdale valley (sometimes spelt Mitredale) and walk there and back. But we're going to suggest a longer walk which takes in some of the other sights in this area. But first the ghost story…

This was originally published by Alice Rea in 1886 but its fame suggests that it was already a local legend. It concerns a couple, Joe and Ann Southward, who lived in a farmhouse near a derelict public house called Nanny Horns in the Miterdale

THE BECKSIDE BOGGLE

valley. One day Joe had to go to Whitehaven on business, not expecting to be back until the next day. Ann stayed at home looking after their 15-month-old child and made up the peat fire to prepare fat for making tallow candles. As night fell there was a loud rap on the door and, on opening it, Ann was greeted by an elderly woman. The lady pleaded to be let in to rest claiming she had walked from Borrowdale and was looking for somewhere to stay the night. The woman had a shawl over her head and refused to remove it saying she had toothache and the warm shawl helped ease the

GET LOST

103

pain. Ann let her in despite being nervous this stranger might be after the horde of money they had hidden away in the house. The lady sat by the fire and Ann made her some milk porridge. With the heat of the fire, both women fell asleep but Ann woke when the kitchen clock struck twelve. She noticed something glinting on the floor near her guest's feet and leaning over realised it was a long, sharp knife. The knife must have fallen from the woman's dress. Ann looked up at the guest and now the shawl had slipped off the face of the sleeping woman to reveal the visage of a man with black bristly stubble. For a moment

GET LOST
104

The path to Miterdale.

Ann was paralysed with fright. But realising the deception, she picked up a ladle and filled it with the boiling fat from the pan on the fire. The man was

sleeping with his mouth wide open and Ann poured the fat down his throat. At first he struggled but she managed to hold him down and the choking, boiling fat soon did its deed. Ann sank back into her own chair and stayed there in shock until her husband returned early the next morning. They decided to bury the body in the ruins of the Nanny Horns and say nothing. They lived for many years with their dreadful secret and on Ann's death bed she confessed to her crime. Could anyone blame her for protecting her home and child? Perhaps not but the spirit of the murdered man is still said to wander the valley, its face still twisted in horrible agony.

Boggle House: The haunted ruins in Miterdale.

THE WALK: The easy and short option is to park in the car park at Miterdale and walk to the ruins. The path takes you through Low Place Farm and a short while after you'll reach the ruins of what is now termed 'Boggle House'. Despite its haunted past, it's a good spot for a picnic before you return to the car park. For those with a bit more stamina, here is our suggested walk:

Park at Eskdale Green (CA19 1TX; Grid Ref: NY141 001) and take the path signposted Giggle Alley. There are public toilets here. If you have time, a short climb up from Giggle

The 'lost' Japanese Garden at Eskdale Green.

Alley takes you to the 'lost' Japanese Garden. It's in a poor state of repair but has a certain magic for being so neglected.

Giggle Alley takes you over the fell and drops you down into Miterdale. Turn right on the road and follow this to Low

GET LOST
106

Place Farm. It's one of those paths where you have to walk through the middle of the farm but fear not, it's a public path and the residents are quite friendly! Just after the farm take the left-hand path (ignoring the sign to 'Hod Reet Fur Eshdel'). You'll pass a building called Bakerstead and shortly after the derelict buildings of Nanny Horns and Boggle House. Enjoy your picnic here, keeping one eye out for any wandering spirits! Cross the beck by the bridge and head up the side of the fell. Once on top you'll need to take a compass bearing (see page 169) to find your way to the stone circles but they are worth seeking out. Continue over the fell and you'll

Hod Reet Fur Eshdel (Head Right for Eskdale) says the sign in Miterdale. But you turn left without crossing the beck.

eventually drop down into Boot. You have a choice of routes back to Giggle Alley. If you turn west just before the fell gate at Boot you can follow the Three Foot Track (a former miners' railway track but now a footpath). Or go into the village of Boot and follow the road to Dalegarth. You can now reward your hard walking

GET LOST

107

with a trip on the Ratty
steam engine back to
Eskdale Green.

FACILITIES: There are
toilets at Giggle Alley
and Dalegarth Station.
There are plenty of places
to eat in the Eskdale
valley including in the
village of Boot or at
Dalegarth Station.

GET LOST 108

Brats Hill
stone circle on
Eskdale
Fell.

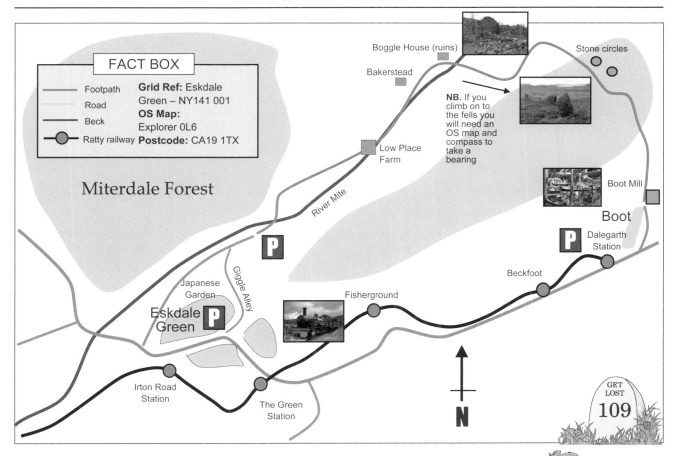

FACT BOX

Footpath
Road
Beck
Ratty railway

Grid Ref: Eskdale Green – NY141 001
OS Map: Explorer 0L6
Postcode: CA19 1TX

Miterdale Forest

Boggle House (ruins)

Stone circles

Bakerstead

NB. If you climb on to the fells you will need an OS map and compass to take a bearing

Low Place Farm

River Mite

Boot Mill

Boot

P

Dalegarth Station

Beckfoot

Japanese Garden

Giggle Alley

Eskdale Green
P

Fisherground

Irton Road Station

The Green Station

N

GET LOST
109

Holy Wells

*"The pilgrims of old knew every holy site and holy well
and felt the sacred everywhere"*

— Fr John Musther

IN the age before tap water (so as late as the early 20th Century in some parts of the UK), water would be obtained from public fountains or natural springs. These provided good clean water, usually all year round. And since it usually came from underground, it had been naturally filtered and was therefore healthy to drink. Some of these springs gained a reputation for being able to cure particular ailments, or became imbued with legends and tales of Saints working miracles at them. These became known as sacred springs or holy wells (though they were always springs rather than the Jack-and-Jill style of well) and were often visited by pilgrims who travelled many miles looking for a health cure or just to pay their respects to the Saint associated with it.

But the arrival of the tap in every household made these sites redundant and they fell into neglect. Most holy wells in

*The wells of rocky Cumberland
Have each a saint or patron,
Who holds an annual festival,
The joy of maid or matron.*

— June Days Dingle

GET
LOST
110

Cumbria are in a poor state but there have been attempts by some enthusiasts to restore or preserve them. In 2014, members of the Orthodox Church in Cumbria, headed by Father John Musther, carried out a large-scale programme of work on a number of our holy wells. The Church has a strong belief in the sanctity of the landscape, including its holy wells. Members of the Church from as far afield as Germany, Iceland, Romania, Slovakia and Turkey restored a number of the wells and now regularly visit them. There are about 200 holy wells in

Father John Musther and volunteers tidying up the holy well at St John's in the Vale.

Previous page: St Andrew's holy well at Kirkandrews-upon-Eden (Grid Ref: NY353585)

GET LOST
112

Cumbria and we've picked out some that are worthy of visiting.

ST CUTHBERT'S WELL, WETHERAL: CA4 8JP (Grid Ref: NY467 548 – pictured opposite). Wetheral is east of Carlisle; take the A69 and cross the M6 (Junction 43); Wetheral is signposted on the right. St Cuthbert is one of Cumbria's local saints and you'll find many churches and sites dedicated to him in the county. This well was last restored in 2001 and shows how something as humble (but important) as a holy well can be made into a beautiful site. It's an ideal spot for a bit of peace and quiet, and a picnic. There are other sites worthy of a visit while you are in Wetheral. For the fit (and youngsters learning to count) you may wish to visit the 99 Steps adjacent to the beautiful Wetheral Station. Are there really 99 steps?

You can then continue your walk along the river to St Constantine's Cells (Grid Ref: NY466 534). These are three caves set beside the River Eden and known to have been used in the 14th Century. Legend says that St Constantine lived here as a hermit. Be aware that there are steps leading down to the caves but otherwise it is a reasonably easy path.

ST JOHN'S IN THE VALE, KESWICK CA12 4UB (Grid Ref: NY306 224): This charming holy well was cleaned up by Fr John

GET LOST
113

Musther and volunteers from the Orthodox Church in 2014 but is generally kept in excellent condition. This church sits at the top of one of the most beautiful valleys in the Lake District and the holy well is to the side of the church. Also nearby you'll find Castle Lonning and Castlerigg stone circle.

ST KENTIGERN'S WELL, CALDBECK CA7 8DT (Grid Ref: NY325 399). Another local Saint is remembered through St Kentigern's Well in Caldbeck. The well is beside the river and is well marked and kept in good condition. St Kentigern is also known by the name St Mungo and a famous

The holy well at St John's in the Vale, near Keswick.

rhyme recalls his miracles:

Here is the bird that never flew
Here is the tree that never grew
Here is the bell that never rang
Here is the fish that never swam

The bird was a robin, killed by Mungo's school mates which he restored to life. The tree was a hazel that Mungo used to relight a fire he had let go out; The bell of St Mungo has been lost but a replica does ring at Glasgow Cathedral. The fish recalls a time Queen Languoreth appealed to St Mungo for help. The king, in a fit of misplaced jealousy, asked her to show him the ring he had given her to prove she had not given it away to some secret lover. But the King had secretly thrown it in the river. On being

GET LOST
114

unable to find the ring, the Queen appealed to Mungo for help. He asked a servant to catch a fish and when the fish was cut open, there was the ring.

ST MARY'S WELL, GOSFORTH

CA20 1BN (Grid Ref: NY071 039). This is a short walk from the village in West Cumbria. Take the path north-east from the church which goes through people's back gardens(!) and then onto the fields. The well is covered by a metal grid and fencing; it would be fantastic to see this well restored one day. Although the well is not much to look at the views from the side of the hill are worth the excursion. (See also p63 for more Gosforth walks).

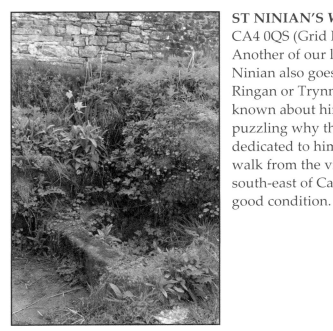

St Kentigern's Well, Caldbeck.

ST NINIAN'S WELL, BRISCO

CA4 0QS (Grid Ref: NY422 519). Another of our local saints. St Ninian also goes by the name Ringan or Trynnian. Little is known about him so it's puzzling why this well is dedicated to him. It's a short walk from the village of Brisco, south-east of Carlisle and is in good condition.

GET LOST

115

- If you wish to hunt out other holy wells in Cumbria, take a look at our Google map (shorturl.at/opBMX). The definitive book on Cumbria's holy wells, *Springs of Living Waters* by Fr John Musther is available from Amazon.

GET LOST 116

Pictured right: St Ninian's holy well at Brisco near Carlisle.

Servants' path

"I cannot see the wit of walking and talking at the same time"

– William Hazlitt

THIS is an easy and very pleasant walk between two idyllic English villages: Maulds Meaburn and Crosby Ravensworth.

We are grateful to author and blogger John Bainbridge in his Walking The Old Ways blog (walkingtheoldways.wordpress.com) for information on this route. It runs from the old manor house of Flass to the church at Crosby Ravensworth

The sign on the church door at Crosby Ravensworth.

but we're suggesting starting at the adjacent village of Maulds Meaburn. The path was created in the 19th Century by the Dent family – the owners of Flass – as a path for the servants to walk to the church (we're guessing the lord of the manor and his family went by horse and carriage!). As Mr Bainbridge says in his blog, "To facilitate their passage, the owners of Flass built two beautiful step stiles in the drystone walls. They're still there today, and I hope they remain safe from the zealots who want every stile destroyed in

GET
LOST
117

favour of gates". To which we echo 'hear, hear'. We want paths to be open to people of all abilities but hope a gate can be added nearby rather than destroying these charming pieces of countryside furniture.

The Dent family traded in tea and opium in the 19th Century so it was perhaps apposite that when police raided Flass in 2012 they found it being used as a cannabis factory. Six men were jailed for their part in the crime. The Grade II listed mansion is privately-owned and currently being restored.

A 'fat man's agony' on the Servants' Path.

START: NY627 160. Maulds Meaburn is on the eastern side of the M6. Park in this charming village but be aware that sheep roam freely here so drive carefully and keep dogs on a lead. The village is in Cumbria but is actually part of the Westmorland Dales and the Yorkshire Dales National Park. Head for the south-east corner and you will see a public footpath signpost which takes you to Flass. You will cross over a cattlegrid and follow the drive towards the mansion. Do not go into the mansion but take the footpath on the left-hand side which hugs the outside of the mansion's wall. You'll pass under a tunnel (pictured opposite) and then head west

GET
LOST
119

across the field. Go through the 'fat man's agony' stile and then after a few yards, the second stile. Follow the river towards Crosby Ravensworth and you will be sure of seeing plenty of wildlife. As you approach Crosby Ravensworth you will go through two red gates; then turn right over Monks Bridge and you will reach the church. A few yards beyond the church you will find the community-owned pub, The Butchers Arms where you can stop for lunch before heading back to Maulds Meaburn.

The pretty village of Maulds Meaburn where sheep freely roam.

OTHER PLACES TO VISIT

GAMELANDS STONE CIRCLE: Postcode CA10 3SE. Grid Ref: NY640 081. One of the lesser known stone circles just a short walk from Orton. Orton and its neighbour Tebay are delightful villages with cafes and pubs. Orton even has its own chocolate factory: Kennedys Fine Chocolates can be found in the centre of the village and it is open to the public as a cafe.

Gamelands stone circle.

DR FARRAR OF ORTON

For just across the Lune's broad stream
A man once lived could solve a dream
Or by the stars could fortunes tell
Circumvent a witch; love philters sell

TEBAY is famous for Mary Baines, a witch who lived there in the 18th Century but less well known is Dr Farrar, a wizard who would have lived in the town around the same time as Mary. He was born in 1681

and died in 1756 at the age of 75. His grave can be found just outside the main door at Orton's All Saints' Church. Some snippets about his life and work have survived but there is more myth than fact. It's known he did write a book about his work and beliefs; the manuscript certainly existed as late as 1856 when Rev James Simpson held it up at a lecture he gave in Kendal on local folklore. It was titled *Dr Farrar's Book of Black Art* and he commented that, "until lately it was believed that there was great danger in opening this book… you might perchance raise the wind and not know how to allay it". Despite the warning he did open it and showed that it dealt with the "motions of the heavenly

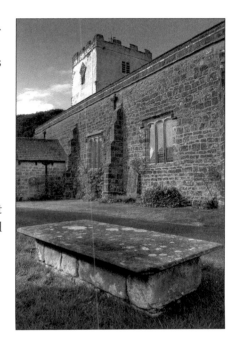

The grave of wizard Dr Farrar at Orton Church.

GET LOST

121

bodies" and how to cast a horoscope but he concluded: "There is not much of any value in the book." Sadly the manuscript has since been lost.

It is often said, however, that Dr Farrar was a good wizard and used his powers to defeat witchcraft and Satanism. *The Monthly Magazine* in 1803 for instance said of him: "If the spouse was jealous that the heart of her husband was estranged from her, she immediately consulted the anti-conjuror (Dr Farrar) and desired him to restore the affections of her bewitched partner. If a friend or relative was confined to the bed of

sickness, relief and convalescence could not be expected without the supernatural assistance and balsamic medicines of Mr Farrar. If a person became deranged in his intellects the injured cells of the brain were to be healed and adjusted by the magic charms of this celebrated man. If a farmer happened to lose his cattle it was necessary to purify the walls of the house with water sprinkled by this famous conjuror; and in endeavouring to account for the latent cause of this disaster, he generally found small parcels of heterogeneous matter deposited in the walls and consisting of the legs of mice and the wings of bats; which he affirmed to be the work of witches. If a person was

desirous of knowing the issue of any event he repaired to Mr Farrar who failed not to satisfy him in this particular."

Historical records prove there was indeed a Dr Farrar who was clearly a much-respected figure in Tebay and Orton but his reputation seems to have become wrapped up in fantastic stories, legends and ballads. Even 100 years after his death, Rev Simpson said: "His doings are still talked about in the locality where he dwelt."

But the vicar of Orton who buried him in 1756 seemed determined to bury the legends along with the man and had this inscription carved on to his

GET LOST
122

tombstone:

"Under this stone lie the remains of Dr William Farrar, of Redgill, whom long experiences rendered eminent in his profession and who was an instance that knowledge in the ways of death doth not exempt from its approach. Reader, in this thy day live well, that thou mayest have hope of a joyful resurrection. He died July 31st 1756, aged 75 yeard".

You can just about make out the inscription on the tombstone which is just outside the church porch.

THE ORTON DOBBIE

Wey Davie hes te heard the news
About the Worton boggle
It's turn'd the clock the wrang side up
And meade the house aw joggle

TEBAY had its witch, Orton had its wizard. And the fells above these towns also had a world-famous ghost. There must surely be some magic in the landscape in this part of Cumbria. The ghost is known as the Orton Dobbie. This dobbie first made its appearance in April 1849 at Cowper's Farm above Tebay – the home of the Gibson family. It might have remained a local mystery but for the fact that a fair was taking place in Orton at the time and word soon got around about the

All that remains of the haunted farmhouse on the fell.

GET LOST
123

strange happenings. The *Kendal Mercury* reported a few days later on the news:

"The first manifestation of ill-will or annoyance, we understand, was the upsetting of a cradle, in which the infant child of Mr Wm. Gibson, the farmer, was sleeping, following this up immediately by causing the chairs, tables, and other articles of furniture to dance about the house floor as if inspired with life, and committing other strange freaks. On one occasion the churn was pulled out of its place by the same invisible hand, and set in motion; on another the

'Of course the stories of the internal parts of the churn and so forth flying through the air are gross fictions, told on the authority, not of eyewitnesses, but agents in the nummery'

milk in the dairy was skimmed and dashed about like the spray of the ocean. In short, at times every article in the house appeared to be revolutionizing."

The news quickly spread across the country and indeed, was

covered by newspapers in other countries. A steady stream of 'boggle-hunters' made their way to the farm and in some cases, were fortunate to witness the phenomena for themselves. The family by this time had fled to stay with relatives. The pressure on the police to 'solve' the case or for the Church to exorcise the ghost grew and it's perhaps little surprise that the dobbie was explained away as a hoax a couple of weeks later:

"We have just heard that the Orton ghost has been laid by a policeman! We are informed that on Thursday last, Mr Slee, a police-officer of Penrith, and another person, after visiting the spot and cross-questioning the

GET LOST

124

aforesaid servant lass, elicited from her that she with the connivance of the 'missus', had been the contriver of all the 'dobbie' work, their motive being a dislike to the house, which is at present very old, and in the vernacular 'ramshackle'. Of course the stories of the internal parts of the churn and so forth flying through the air are gross fictions, told on the authority, not of eyewitnesses, but agents in the nummery."

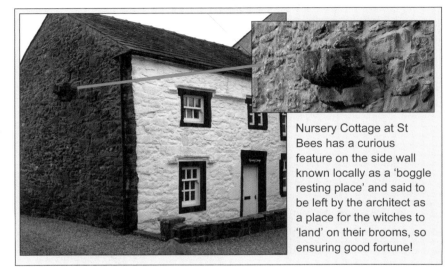

Nursery Cottage at St Bees has a curious feature on the side wall known locally as a 'boggle resting place' and said to be left by the architect as a place for the witches to 'land' on their brooms, so ensuring good fortune!

But this dobbie was not going to go away so quietly. A few days later the maid and family made it clear that the policeman had threatened her unless she 'confessed' to it being a hoax. Besides many witnesses had seen things happen despite none of the family even being in the farmhouse.

The excitement continued for some weeks before fizzling out. But we have spoken to one elderly lady who recalled as a child going up to the ruins of Cowper's Farm to pick up stones because it was believed they contained magical properties. The farm no longer exists.

GET LOST
125

On the towpath

"It is a pleasure to meet the man who has learned the art of going slowly"

— Stephen Graham, The Gentle Art of Tramping

ASK most people about canals in Cumbria and they'll be hard-pressed to think of any, and although our county is not as well endowed with these magical waterways as the Midlands, we can lay claim to at least three. The great appeal of the canal environment is its almost hidden nature. You know it is there, but access is by way of narrow gaps at

the side of the canal bridge, or an innocuous gap in the hedge leading to the towpath – like a

secret door leading to an almost magical domain. That magic includes, not only pleasant, de-stressing canalside walks with all its wildlife and industrial history spotting, but also the opportunity to take the family on a trip on a canal boat. Anyone in Ulverston will point you towards their canal (pictured left) with its long, straight and wheelchair/pushchair friendly towpath. The leisurely walk stretches from Canal Head just

GET LOST
126

Walk down Kirkbie Green

Cross Miller Bridge

KENDAL

Towpath starts by recycling centre

Kendal Castle

Natland Road

Walk along Natland Road for a few yards before rejoining the towpath

River Kent

NATLAND

outside the delightful town centre to the coast of Morecambe Bay at the appropriately-named Canal Foot, and welcome refreshment at the Bay Horse Hotel. Industrial archaeology buffs will appreciate the canal's unique rolling railway bridge and the ghost-like remains of the lock gates.

Boasting a much longer canal in the northernmost part of the county was Port Carlisle. Its canal was over 11 miles long and

GET LOST
128

took sailing boats into the heart of the city of Carlisle but only the merest ghost of that rich industrial past is visible now.

It's further south at Crooklands that we find the best-surviving Cumbrian canal stretches. The Lancaster Canal officially ends at Tewitfield where the M6 rudely halts its progress but short stretches of the old Lancaster Canal that once linked with Kendal have survived. And it's on these Cumbrian stretches that you can even enjoy regular canal boat excursions aboard

Waterwitch (pictured p127). You can start at either end of the canal for our suggested towpath walk: Kendal or Crooklands. Kendal offers the facilities provided by a bustling town, and Crooklands offers you the opportunity to see Waterwitch in operation. At Crooklands you will also find a hotel just opposite Waterwitch's mooring with good facilities for food and drink, and friendly staff. Heading west from Crooklands, there comes a point at Stainton Bridge End where the canal completely dries up but you can

Larkrigg Spring woods

Sedgwick

A590

Once through Larkrigg Spring woods you follow the dried-up canal which includes some remaining bridges

Drop down to the main road and turn left following the road over the A590 for a short time. Rejoin the footpath as it cuts through woods on your left

follow the towpath all the way to Kendal. There are places where the path takes a slight detour but it's an intriguing walk offering a glimpse of a lost age.

STARTING from Kendal, it's easy to follow the towpath even though the canal was drained of water many years ago. The canal reached into the town centre and you can still see the ghosts of this once important water highway. Park in Kendal and it's a short walk over the river across Miller Bridge to the start of the towpath walk. There are a number of cut-throughs to what is now a popular cyclepath and footpath but if you want to join at the very start of the former canal, walk up Kirkbie Green to the town's recycling centre. On the right of this is a footpath – and the start of the canal walk. Despite this inauspicious start, you'll soon be able to pick out the former route of the canal as you walk along the towpath through a mixture of houses, allotments and light industrial units. Just to reassure you, every now and again you'll see a canal bridge still standing – even if it has no water to cross. You will eventually reach Natland Road. Walk just a few yards along this and then cross the road to rejoin the towpath walk. It is signposted but the signpost can get overgrown so keep a careful eye out. You continue along a wooded path and another canal bridge will reassure you that

GET LOST
129

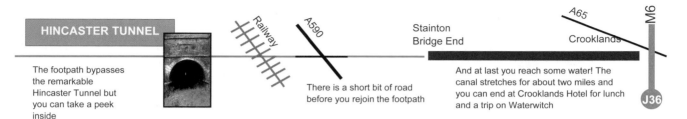

HINCASTER TUNNEL

The footpath bypasses the remarkable Hincaster Tunnel but you can take a peek inside

Railway

A590

There is a short bit of road before you rejoin the footpath

Stainton Bridge End

Crooklands

A65

M6

J36

And at last you reach some water! The canal stretches for about two miles and you can end at Crooklands Hotel for lunch and a trip on Waterwitch

you are still on the right route. It then opens out into fields as it continues its route towards Crooklands. At all times the route is clear and for much of it you will be able to make out the dips in the ground that once housed the busy canal. In addition to the bridges, you can also spot the occasional milestone – looking rather odd in the middle of a field. You'll

GET LOST
130

pass the remarkable Hincaster Tunnel before crossing over the A590 and rejoining the towpath until you reach Stainton Bridge End and the welcome sight of the canal with water in in it! Follow the towpath to Crooklands where you can hop aboard Waterwitch (see p132) or call into the Crooklands Hotel for some welcome refreshment.

Pictured right: The former canal is now a well-made path

FACT BOX

————	Road
————	Towpath
————	Canal
————	M-way

Grid Ref:
Kendal – SD519 926
Crooklands – SD531 836

OS Map:
Explorer OL7

Postcode:
Kendal – LA9 7BY
Crooklands – LA7 7NH

ORIGINALLY the Lancaster Canal stretched 57 miles from Preston to Kendal, and was highly successful for some years. Falling into decline due to the threat posed by the railway companies, the last commercial load was carried on the canal in 1947. In the 1960s the northward extension of the M6 led to culverting the Lancaster Canal in several places to accommodate the new road. Now only 42 miles are navigable, but the few miles of reserve canal north of Tewitfield are still open for walking, fishing, cycling, canoeing and an occasional trailboat festival.

All aboard Waterwitch which offers trips along the last remaining stretch of canal.

GET LOST

132

Waterwitch

NARROWBOAT Waterwitch is owned and operated by the Lancaster Canal Trust and manned by volunteers. She operates from Crooklands Bridge, just off the A65, every Sunday and Bank Holiday from the beginning of May to the end of September, and each Saturday in August as well. There are further mid-week trips arranged on Westmorland Show day as the canal runs right alongside the showground. For just a few pounds passengers can enjoy a 45-minute chug up the canal from just south of Crooklands Bridge (number 166 for canal aficionados) to just beyond Mattinson's Bridge, number 168, and back again. Travelling at 4mph enables you to relax and enjoy the wildlife close up.

Packhorse bridges

"There is a pleasure in the pathless woods"

— Lord Byron

THINK of the Lake District and you think of its fells, lakes and packhorse bridges. These tiny but well-made bridges have often survived for centuries – and unlike most modern bridges have actually improved with age. The iconic Ashness Bridge above Derwentwater has featured on postcards, biscuit tin lids and chocolate box covers for

Row Bridge, Wasdale.

decades thanks to its beautiful setting. It's certainly well worth

a visit; it's just a short trip from Keswick – we recommend travelling on the launch over Derwentwater and then it's a short walk up the well-made road. And you can go on from there to Surprise View or even on to Watendlath. But this book is about avoiding the popular or cliche and there are hundreds

GET LOST
133

of other packhorse bridges in Cumbria to choose from; we're going to point you in the direction of just a few.

ROW BRIDGE, WASDALE
CA20 1EX. (Grid Ref: NY186 089): The fragile-looking bridge (see picture on previous page) stretches over Mosedale Beck behind the Wasdale Head Inn. Its official name is Row Bridge but most people know it just as Wasdale Head packhorse bridge. This valley (voted Britain's Favourite View in 2007) is the jumping-off point for those climbing Scafell Pike (England's highest mountain) so it can be busy. Choose a quieter day of the week and take a

GET LOST
134

The impossible-looking Monk's Bridge crosses Friars Gill near Calder Bridge, West Cumbria but it is better known locally as Matty Benn's Bridge. Matty was Martha Benn (born 1831) who lived at Brackenthwaite Farm, Wilton with husband John. She would regularly return home from market on horseback and drunk, precariously crossing the bridge. Descendant Geoff Benn says: "The locals began to refer to the bridge as Matty Benn's Bridge and the name sticks to this day." She died in 1888. Grid Ref: NY063 101. Src: loweswatercam.co.uk.

Pictured opposite: The remarkable double packhorse bridge at Wasdale Head. Grid Ref: NY183 065

GET LOST

135

picnic to enjoy by the lake.

DOUBLE PACKHORSE BRIDGE, Wasdale CA20 1EX (Grid Ref: NY183 065). While you are in Wasdale, take a short walk on the corpse road heading to Burnmoor Tarn and Eskdale and you'll come across an unusual double packhorse bridge.

HIGH SWEDEN BRIDGE, Ambleside LA22 9BB (Grid Ref: NY379 067). This bridge – pictured on p137 – is part of a circular walk from Ambleside and is among our favourites because you'll often see the friendly giant Highland cattle roaming on the

fellside. You can head out on the path leading through the Ambleside campus of the University of Cumbria on the northern edge of the town. This often opens its car park to the public and, as it's lesser known, often has parking spaces when others in the town have filled up. Also here you will find the wonderful Mary Armitt Museum which we highly recommend you visit on your trip to Ambleside. Follow that path up to the bridge and then cross over and return through Rough Sides Wood and you'll eventually arrive back in the town centre. Be aware it is a good path but a steep one so is not a route for those who might find the going tough. When you

The Fairy Drinking Well near High Sweden Bridge, Ambleside. Grid Ref: NY379 063.

walk through Rough Sides Wood you will pass the Fairy Drinking Well but it's not signposted and is very difficult to find. This natural spring achieved local fame for its apparent healing qualities – and that fairies drank from it. Watch out for a couple of small quarry workings in Rough Sides Wood – the spring flows from rocks to be found just at the southern end of the quarry; it's by the path and unusually for a spring is a couple of feet from ground level. One former resident recalls she was told fairies could "lean over and drink straight from it". Others tell how people have sworn by its healing properties – but we wouldn't recommend drinking the water. There is a

GET
LOST
137

tradition of fairies living close to Ambleside and according to an account written by HS Cowper in 1897, the fairy folk could easily mingle with humans. Cowper noted: "Thus I learned from one old inhabitant that in his young days he heard strange stories of the doings of these folks (fairies) in the fairs and market at Ambleside, and elsewhere. In the guise of ordinary folks they would mix with the crowds, and then, by blowing at the market women at the stalls, they became invisible, after which, taking a mean advantage of their position, they proceeded to steal things off the stalls."

Stagshaw Garden,
Ambleside LA22 0HE
(Grid Ref: NY379 028).

Ambleside is one of the more popular Lake District towns and, with its location close to Lake Windermere, has plenty to offer. But can we recommend one of the lesser known attractions: Stagshaw Garden can be found opposite the Hayes Garden Centre. It is maintained by the National Trust and is a quiet haven in an otherwise busy tourist town. That said, you will occasionally see and hear low-flying military jets go over Lake Windermere but Common Wood is an excellent viewpoint to see and photograph the jets. They fly low enough for you to be able to wave at the pilots!

Footpath names

"No man who uses a map need grow old"

— H H Symonds

CUMBRIA has a rich vocabulary when it comes to footpaths. The need in the past to know how wide a path was, how steep it was and even if you could get your horse up it, led to numerous names each with a specific definition. They start with a sheep's trod which is the first hint of a path that is created by sheep returning to the farm.

As humans follow this track, the path becomes widened. If it leads to a farm it might be called a lonning (the loan was 'the quiet place by the farm' where villagers could buy milk, eggs or other farm produce); if the path climbed a hill it might be a

GET LOST
139

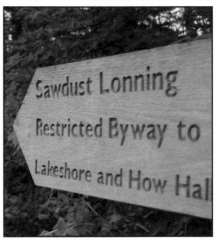

Paraffin Alley can be found in Keswick. Sawdust Lonning is in Ennerdale.

rake; if it crossed an estuary it would be a wath and so on. Important or popular paths also took on individual names and it's in this regard that Cumbria seems to excel. Most are nicknames known only to the locals so you won't normally see a signpost pointing them out. Some are quite logical: Mackenzies

GET LOST 140

Lonning led to Mr Mackenzie's mine while Johnnie Bulldog's Lonning got its name from Johnnie MacElroy who lived with his bulldog in this Carlisle lonning in the 1880s. Others are more subtle: The many Lovers Lonnings were named because these were paths favoured by the romantics in the village; Squeezed Gut Lonning (there are several in Cumbria) indicates

the narrowness of the paths and Nanny Knockabouts because this is where parents would leave their children to 'knockabout'.

We thought we would share some of the more intriguing and delightful names of the county's paths for you to ponder over…

GIGGLE ALLEY

ANNE'S WALK

FAT MAN'S AGONY

SLACK RANDY

CRAGGY BUTTS

THIEF STREET

BLOODY BONES LANE

OLD MOSES TROD

LANTY SLEE PATH

WILLIE OF THE BOATS

ETTERBY WATH

BLACK SHIP

PARSON'S PASSAGE

WALK-HER-HOME LANE

SQUEEZED GUT LONNING

CHITTY MOUSE PATH

BLUEBOTTLE LONNING

TICKLEBELLY ALLEY

DONKEY TROD

ALLY'S ASS

THE RASH

TRODDEN BIT

99 STEPS

DANDY WALK

COFFIN ROUTE

CINDER PATH

T'CRACK

DICK TROD LANE

GET LOST

141

Taking the long way home

THIS book is mainly concerned with short walks along ancient paths but there are in Cumbria a number of long distance paths for the more determined walker. The most famous is perhaps the **Coast 2 Coast** walk which starts at St Bees and reaches across Cumbria before heading to the east coast (see page 73). **Hadrian's Wall** path also crosses the country west to east. The **Cumbria Way** crosses the county north to south, covering a distance of around 80 miles and linking up shorter footpaths en route. There is a **Cumbria Coastal Way** which takes you along the coast but at times has to come some distance inland. Most lakes have a circular path and one of the more recent to be marked out is the **Ullswater Way** – a 20-mile ramble around the lake. There are some which mark out an historic trail even if it's not a true ancient path. So **Isaac's Tea Trail** starting at Alston honours an itinerant tea seller. And **Lady Anne's Way** is a 100-mile route honouring Lady Anne Clifford who travelled between her two castles at Skipton and Brougham, near Penrith. In the south of the county there is the **Cistercian Way** which takes in the Furness and Cartmel peninsulas. In addition to these you will find a number of shorter walks marked out by district councils and tourist bodies. Watch out also for annual sponsored walks such as the **Keswick to Barrow** walk which offer organised events.

Our treacherous waths

"The Kent and Keer have swallowed many a man and his mare"

— local saying

THERE is one type of path you will find in Cumbria which is just too dangerous for us to detail: Waths. A wath is a ford across an estuary and although they are effectively redundant now a few still exist as recognised footpaths and we have also come across unofficial ones known only to the local residents. But crossing an estuary is a dangerous business and we're not going to advise anyone attempts them

unless they have a guide. A number of waths cross the

Solway Estuary to Scotland but evidence of the dangers is provided by the loss of the army of Scottish King, Alexander II, which was overwhelmed by the fast-approaching tide as the soldiers tried to cross the wath in 1216, resulting in the drowning of 1,900 men.

The most famous wath is to the south of the county, crossing

GET LOST

143

Morecambe Bay. The Queen appoints a guide to help people cross this potentially lethal bay's quicksands and tidal courses. The Queen's Guide to the Sands was first appointed in 1548 and the latest holder of the post is Michael Wilson who hosts occasional guided walks across the bay for groups of people (usually charity fundraisers). Visit www.guideoversands.co.uk for details of guided walks over the Sands. The Queen's Guide to the Sands is only paid £15 a year although he is able to stay rent-free in a cottage on Kents Bank. But it's a cottage that was only recently modern-ised to include electricity and

The warning at the start of the Ravenglass wath.

running water; the previous occupant Cedric Robinson had to make do with a gas lamp. Mr Robinson described the wath as the "most dangerous highway in Britain". The Broomway in Essex (another path across an estuary) might dispute that but it's fair to say both have a long and deadly history of claiming the lives of over-confident walkers. Modern deaths of people getting caught out in Morecambe Bay are not unknown.

Waths offer not only a valuable short-cut for travellers but also a route for invading armies to make a surprise attack and centuries of troubles in the Borderland between Scotland and England has seen much use

GET LOST

144

made of the waths crossing the Solway Estuary. You can find out more about them on the Solway Shore-walker blog of Ann Lingard or her website, solwayshorestories.co.uk. She writes: "Although it's difficult these days to identify the various waths other than through historical accounts, partly because the topography of the shores and marshes have changed so dramatically, the three main waths were the Sulwath across the mouth of the River Esk, the Peatwath across the River Eden, and the Bowness wath across the Firth. There was also the Dornock or Sandy Wath

The footpath over the wath at Ravenglass includes a tide table.

PATH LIABLE TO TIDAL FLOODING
For tides above 7.2m for 2 hours
before and after high water.
Check tide tables

GET
LOST
145

across a broad stretch of the Firth from Drumburgh to Dornock; Blawath a little further to the east; and shorter waths – Rockcliffe Wath and Stoney Wath – across the Eden, and Loanwath across the Sark". (It should be noted that this is a reference to the River Esk near Carlisle not the other River Esk near Ravenglass). R. S. Ferguson writing in 1885 in the *Transactions of the Cumberland and Westmorland Antiquarian and Archaeological Society* also referenced a Rockcliffe Wath "a little below Rockcliffe Church" and an Etterby Wath crossing the Eden. Ferguson noted the Waths were all but forgotten and,

A friend stops to say hello at the start of Waberthwaite Wath near Ravenglass.

given the nature of the shifting sands in estuaries we again advise **not** trying to walk these ancient paths. But that said there's no doubt that a walk along the Solway or Ravenglass estuaries will provide you with an exhilarating walk with astonishing views and much wildlife to spot.

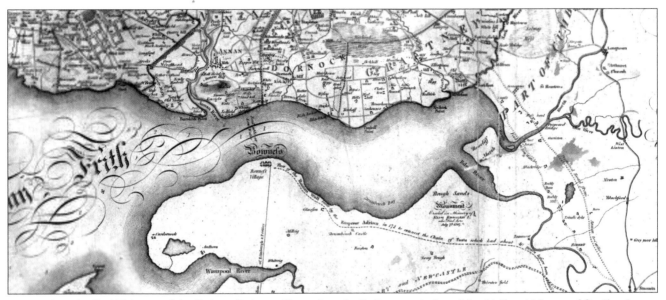

William Crawford's 1804 map of the Solway Estuary. *Reproduced with the permission of the National Library of Scotland*

There was also a famous ford at a spot called Greenbed but better known as Willie of the Boats. WT McIntire writing in *CWAAS* transactions (1939) noted: "The ford of Willie of the Boats acquired in the days of the Gretna Green romances a certain romantic interest of its own, for it was frequently employed by run-away couples, who in their haste to escape from their pursuers, chose this hazardous

GET LOST

147

short cut to Gretna in preference to the longer but safer road round by Longtown. They were sometimes foiled, we are told, by the vagaries of the Solway tide, and had to wait impatiently beside the Esk fearing every moment to be overtaken by an irate parent."

Willie was apparently one William Irving and a verse attributed to Robert Burns tells:

Here gentlemen, you have a guide
To either Scotch or English side,
And you need never fear the tide,
When with the boatman,
With horse or drove he'll with you ride.

Esk Boathouse and the plaque honouring Willie of the Boats.

An epitaph to Willie of the Boats is still recorded on a plaque at Esk Boathouse at Rockcliffe (NY340 637)

The waths across the Esk Estuary near Ravenglass are still shown on Ordnance Survey maps and their dangerous character and mirky past have given rise to a number of fatalities and warning stories. Mary Bragg for instance was found drowned in the estuary in 1805 and her boggle (ghost) still haunts the area. More famously Thomas Skelton or Tom the Fool, a wicked 16th Century jester who lived at Muncaster Castle which still sits above the estuary, delighted in sending travellers on the wrong path over the estuary so they would succumb to the quicksands. He would sit under a chestnut tree by the castle – the tree still survives – awaiting gullible walkers who would ask him for directions. You can also see Tom's portrait in the castle and each year the castle appoints a

Tom Skelton: Castle jester and unreliable guide to the sands.

jester to entertain visitors. John Wesley, the founder of the Methodist movement, crossed

the estuary in 1759 so fortunately didn't have to contend with the dubious navigational skills of Tom Fool but he did have to deal with the 'generation of liars' who lived at Ravenglass and seemed determined to thwart his attempts to cross the wath:

"**Saturday, May 12:** Setting out early from Flookburgh, we came to Bootle about 24 measured miles from Flookburgh, soon after eight, having crossed the Millom Sand (Duddon Sands) without either guide or difficulty. Here we were informed that we could not pass at Ravenglass before one or

GET LOST

149

two o'clock; whereas, had we gone on, as we afterwards found, we might have passed immediately. About eleven we were directed to a ford near Muncaster Hall, which they said we might cross at noon. When we came thither, they told us we could not cross; so we sat till about one. We then found we could have crossed at noon. However, we reached Whitehaven before night. But I have taken my leave of the sand road. I believe it is ten measured miles shorter than the other (ie overland by Kendal and Dunmail Raise) but there are four sands to pass so far from each other, that it is scarce possible to pass

GET LOST 150

'I can advise no stranger to go this way. He may go round by Kendal and Keswick, often in less time, always with less expense, and far less trial of his patience'

– John Wesley

them all in a day; especially as you have all the way to do with a generation of liars, who delay all strangers as long as they can, either for their own gain or their neighbours'. I can advise no stranger to go this way. He may

go round by Kendal and Keswick, often in less time, always with less expense, and far less trial of his patience." *

The waths may be too dangerous to walk but there are many wonderful paths along the Solway and Ravenglass estuaries you can walk.

* From Wesley's diaries. With grateful thanks to Paul Hindle's book, *Roads and Tracks of the Lake District* for the story.

Our thanks also to David Livermore and solwayshorewalker.wordpress.com

Pictured opposite: Tom the Fool's tree in front of Muncaster Castle.

GET
LOST
151

If you're walking along the Ravenglass Estuary, here are some places to visit…

GET LOST 152

THE LA'AL RATTY

THIS little steam engine runs throughout the year from Ravenglass to Dalegarth. It was a railway originally used by miners operating in Eskdale but has now been taken over by steam rail enthusiasts. The gift shops sell books and leaflets detailing walks from the stations along the 40-minute route.

At Ravenglass you will find a museum telling the history of the railway. There are cafes at Ravenglass and Dalegarth (Boot) stations.

MUNCASTER CASTLE

THE castle has been home to the Pennington family for 900 years and is open to the public. There are a number of events throughout the year, including at the end of May a festival at which the jester is appointed for the next year. Hopefully none of them repeat the trick of Tom the Fool and send travellers over the wrong estuary path! The gardens are also open to the public and in early May the bluebells put on a stunning display.

The path to church

"There is always further to go"

– Katie Hale, My Name Is Monster

THERE are a number of paths in the county that have allegedly (or actually) been created by members of the clergy. Just as the postman needed paths to go about his business and so created short-cuts, so too the local vicar was known to add an extra path onto the parish map through his excursions. And there are a few Monks' Paths too

'Thin Places: Those rare locales where the distance between heaven and Earth collapses'

suggesting a tradition dating back many centuries. There is something evocative about a path created by one of God's spiritual servants. It's suggestive of a route that embodies the

prayer and solemnity of the vicar on his walk. There are perhaps echoes of the Celtic Christian concept of 'Thin Places' which author Eric Weiner described as "those rare locales where the distance between heaven and Earth collapses". Or as someone else once said, "the places in the world

GET LOST

153

where the walls are weak". We've collected a few such paths which you may wish to walk to share the spiritual solace – or just to enjoy a nice walk.

PARSON'S PASSAGE, ESKDALE

Grid Ref: NY174 004

For a long time this was known officially as Vicar's Walk but the local nickname, Parson's Passage, has won out. It runs from the old vicarage in Eskdale (where newsreader Anna Ford was born) to St Catherine's

Right: Parson's Passage in Eskdale.

Church. From Dalegarth station (home to the La'al Ratty steam engine) turn right onto the main road. Take the first left at the war memorial and after a hundred yards or so you will see a footpath on your left. Parson's Passage is sign-posted on the gate. The 15-minute walk takes you to Church Lonning (part of the old corpse road from Wasdale) to St Catherine's Church. It's a charming church with plenty of interest.

PARSON'S ROAD, ULPHA

Grid Ref: SD202 912

To help you, there is now a signpost at the start of this walk

The start of Parson's Road at Ulpha.

which says "Parson's Road" but 'road' seems too modern a term and the path has previously been called Priest's Walk or Parson's Path which seem much more appropriate terms. The path was created by the late 18th Century vicar of Ulpha Church, Hugh Hodgson. He lived at Stonestar (where the path begins) but also ran a school at Woodland in the next valley. To enable him to short-cut his walk to the school he created a path out of the valley opposite his home. As BS Wignall Simpson records in the 1934 history of the church (*A Mountain Chapelry*), "A way up the gully and over the fell considerably reduced the

GET LOST

155

GET
LOST
156

distance which he had to travel". Rev Hodgson was vicar from 1771 to 1775 but the path has survived the centuries. It was recorded on the early 19th Century maps as Parson's Path and is still noted on Ordnance Survey maps as a public footpath. You can carry on the path to Woodlands if you wish to reach the hostelries of Broughton Mills or Broughton. Indeed, you may wish to park at Broughton and complete the route to Parson's Road in reverse.

There are some who wrongly credit 'Wonderful Walker' with this path. The Rev Robert Walker was an 18th Century vicar but of the neighbouring

Seathwaite parish. He was a vicar of some renown, living a sparse and frugal life full of good works. He was an inspiration for the poet William Wordsworth who said of him:

"Whose good works formed an endless retinue,
A pastor such as Chaucer's verse portrays,
Such as the heaven-taught skill of Herbert drew
And tender Goldsmith crowned with deathless praise."

This cheeky chappy was spotted on Monk's Trod, Castle Carrock.

MONK'S TROD, CASTLE CARROCK

Grid Ref: NY557 555

This is the local name for a path that goes through Hynam Wood near Castle Carrock and, it has been suggested, may have had some connection with Lanercost Priory. The priory is about six miles away and well worth a visit.

Parking: We recommend parking in the parking space adjacent to Jockey Shield Cottage (postcode CA8 9NF). From here it is a short walk down hill to the River Gelt. The path

GET LOST
157

GET
LOST
158

is well made but is a little steep. You can enjoy your *bait* or picnic by the river and watch out for the wildlife including nuthatches and red squirrels. Once over the bridge turn left (west) and the path makes a slow rise up on to Talkin Fell. It's this first part of the path that is known as Monk's Trod but you may wish to walk on further and explore. There is a display board by Jockey Shield Cottage and you'll also find a detailed work on the web courtesy of Mark Richards (just Google 'Monk's Trod Cumbria').

Previous page: Monk's Trod at Castle Carrock in its autumn glory

PRIEST'S WALK, KIRKOSWALD

Grid Ref: NY554 410
Postcode: CA10 1DQ
Parking: Please park considerately in the village.

This is a path to St Oswald's Church and the name, Priest's Walk, may be related to a College for training priests that once existed in the village. It's a 500-yard walk on a flagstone path which is just glorious in autumn (pictured on page 160) but be aware the path is uneven and can get slippery. The church dates back nearly 900 years and is well worth a visit – don't miss the ornate holy well on the western wall. There are a

The holy well with drinking cup.

number of other features to watch out for including the ancient yew trees and a consecration cross. It's a charming place to visit with Penrith or other villages nearby offering places to eat or drink.

GET LOST
159

GET
LOST
160

The Run With No Name

WE have already discovered waths – those estuary paths that are only to be found for a few hours each day. But also in Cumbria are some paths that only exist for a few days each year. These include such exotic names as Outer Mongolia, The Run With No Name, Way Out West and L'eau Noir. They are ski runs to be found on Helvellyn and have been created by the Lake District Ski Club – a club that has been in existence since 1936. The club operates a tow on Raise above Glenridding

Tackling paths that only appear for a few weeks each year.
Picture: Richard Sims

but ski enthusiasts should be fit enough to make the steep climb up carrying their gear and be well-equipped for a mountain environment. You can join the club for an annual fee or pay a daily rate as a guest. You will find more information on ldscsnowski.co.uk including a map of all the ski runs.

GET LOST
161

Life on the edge

Keep your eyes peeled for Cumbria's roadside curiosities

IN the 19th Century Scaw Lonning was a beautiful tree-lined path that young lovers no doubt wandered down on a summer's evening. It stretched from High Harrington, near Workington, towards Winscales Moor – or what we call today, Lillyhall. But in the 20th Century, the motor car arrived and it wasn't long before Scaw Lonning became Scaw Road.

The grave of Joseph Thompson – and his thumb (Grid Ref: NY009 259).

Today it's a busy rat-run which most people speed through to get to work or get back home again.

And yet, look closely, and you'll find an intriguing reminder of days gone by: The gravestone of Joseph Thompson's thumb. In fact the rest of Joseph Thompson is buried there too but it's his thumb for which he will be remembered. The story begins in 1744 when Joseph injured his thumb. The wound became infected and eventually the thumb had to be cut off. He held onto it however and asked the vicar if it might be buried in the parish graveyard so that when the day came for his burial he would be reunited with it. The vicar refused such a bizarre request so Joseph sneaked into the graveyard at night and secretly buried the thumb. But over the next few days, Joseph began to experience tremendous pain in his hand and became convinced it was because he'd angered God by defying the vicar. Joseph's wife sneaked back to the graveyard one night to dig the thumb back up and it was re-buried on Joseph's own land, adjacent to Scaw Lonning. Joseph made it clear he wanted nothing more to do with the Church and that when he died he wanted to be reunited with his thumb in his field. He died a year later and his wish was fulfilled. A gravestone erected in the field included the inscription:

"Joseph Thompson may here be found, Who would not lie in consecrated ground. Died May 13th 1745. Aged 63 when he was alive."

Many years later a tenant working the field spoke to John Christian Curwen, then squire of Workington Hall about the gravestone stuck in the middle of the land making it inconvenient to work the field. Upon being told that the stone marked the grave of a man who refused to be buried in consecrated ground, Curwen said: "Plough him up damn him, plough him up." The gravestone was duly dug up and moved to the hedgerow where it can still be seen today.

Even if they get moved, roadside memorials tend to survive for centuries out of respect for the dead. Those who drive over the Irton fell road will almost certainly fail to see a small roadside memorial to one William Malkinson. Even those walking this route can easily miss it. But it proclaims what some might consider a rather sobering, even chilling warning: "Be Ye Also Ready". In fact that's a Biblical quote and Mr Malkinson was

163

a popular preacher who died aged 51 on February 26, 1866 while walking from Cleator Moor to Eskdale – an impressive 18-mile walk. But he did it while also wearing – for reasons unknown – two waistcoats, two shirts and two coats. As the coroner later said, "sufficient clothes to embarrass and make the breathing more difficult, even on level ground". The doctor suggested the heavy clothing and long walk put an intolerable strain on Mr Malkinson causing him to "expire with terrible suddenness". But he was well-loved and the memorial was erected at the spot he fell

GET LOST

164

Be Ye Also Ready. The memorial for Mr Malkinson (Grid Ref: NY118 012).

with the warning to passers-by that death may come calling at any time and to make sure they are also ready. The memorial is still looked after by locals and by descendants of his family.

Roadside paraphernalia also includes many old-style milestones that some parts of Cumbria care for particularly well even though their use has been overtaken by the age of the sat-nav. Some are particularly idiosyncratic. For example, at Shap you will find one that employs a curious mix of Roman and Arabic numerals to tell you that Kendal is X6 (ie 16) miles away. Life may get even more confusing for the modern traveller at Kirkby Stephen where a signpost gives distances in miles and furlongs. Between Braithwaite and Portinscale is a milestone that boasts an accuracy even sat-nav would struggle to achieve. It proudly claims that London is precisely 290 and a half miles away (it doesn't actually say in which direction). It's hard not to smile when one thinks of the 18th Century workman who, on

The coffin rest at Lamplugh (Grid Ref: NY080 207).

The astonishingly accurate milestone near Keswick (Grid Ref: NY244 235).

being asked to paint a milestone giving the distance from London dreamed up such an impressive calculation! And how would anyone know he was wrong?

We have mentioned earlier in this book the holy wells that you can find scattered around Cumbria's countryside and among the other relics of a more religious age are coffin rests and roadside crosses. These date from medieval times when corpse roads (see page 87) were used to take the dead from remote parishes to the 'mother' church. En route would be coffin rests – roadside crosses or large stones that were stopping points where prayers were said or hymns sung. It's impossible to

GET
LOST
165

say today how many of the claimed coffin rests are genuine but there are some impressive structures. One of the best is between Lamplugh Mill and Low Mill Gill Head. It is now enclosed in a private garden but stands next to the public road so is easy to view (see picture on page 165).

Perhaps equally as old are a number of plague stones. These were used when whole villages were quarantined due to the plague. The food was delivered to the boundary and the villagers left the money in a vinegar-filled well in the stone to disinfect it. You will

The Spillers Stone at Greystoke (Grid Ref: NY443 308).

find a particularly impressive example at Penrith (Grid Ref: NY519 295) but there's also one at Greystoke known as the Spillers Stone. And we suspect

the Spitting Stone at Caldbeck (see page 36) is also a former plague stone that has now been set into a drystone wall.

There is so much to be discovered just lying around our county's 'edges'. And not just on countryside footpaths. Even in our town centres long-redundant signposts survive – often simply because no one has bothered to take them down. Walk along a town centre high street and the ground floor is often a mish-mash of different commercial frontages fighting for your attention. But look up to the second or third storey and you'll often find architecture untouched for a hundred or more years. Ornate plasterwork, ancient light fittings, street signs and more are there waiting to be rediscovered. Just remember to keep your eyes open when out walking and you could make your own discoveries.

The road sign at Kirkby Stephen gives distances in miles and furlongs.

GET LOST

167

Don't get lost

"When in doubt believe not yourself but use your compass"

— H H Symonds

W E have with tongue firmly in cheek called this book, *Get Lost*. But we sincerely hope that is the last thing you will do. The Lake District fells can be deceptive but you should avoid the temptation to just dash up the fellside and instead prepare properly even if you are just heading

GET LOST
168

on an afternoon walk. Check the advice on mountain rescue websites. This includes registering your mobile phone number before you start walking, leaving details of your proposed route and expected time of return with someone, taking equipment (and knowing how to use it) and wearing appropriate clothing. It's good practice to get into the habit of

following this advice even on short walks. Take time to learn how to use a map and compass (YouTube has some helpful videos). In particular it is important to know how to take a bearing. On the fells there are often no signposts and no visible footpaths. By taking a bearing you can ensure you are walking in the right direction. We have printed a guide on p169. This is the one key navigational skill that can save you hours of frustration and possibly your life.

Be aware that the weather can change quickly and be drastically different even climbing a few metres in height. And if you do get into serious trouble and need Mountain Rescue, dial 999 and ask for Cumbria Police, then for the Mountain Rescue Service.

Remember always tell someone where you are going and what time you expect to be back. Then if anything goes wrong they can advise Mountain Rescue which route to search.

Taking A Bearing

FIRST, GET TO KNOW YOUR COMPASS

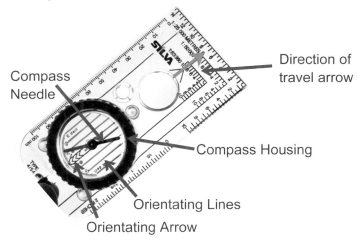

Compass Needle

Direction of travel arrow

Compass Housing

Orientating Lines

Orientating Arrow

Note: Over longer distances you may need to adjust the compass a degree or two for magnetic north (see ordnancesurvey.co.uk) but this is unnecessary on the short paths we describe in this book.

GET LOST
169

1

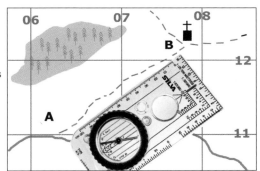

Place compass on the map along your intended route.

2

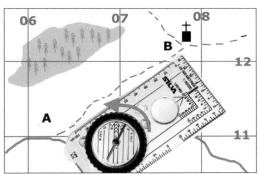

Rotate housing so Orientating Lines line up with the blue gridlines on the map.

1. Line up your compass along the path or route you wish to travel with the Direction Arrow pointing in the direction you wish to go.

2. Rotate the Compass Housing until the Orientating Arrow and Lines are parallel with the blue gridlines on the map.

3 With Orientating Arrow and Compass Needle lined up (circled in red below) the Direction Arrow will point you in the direction you need to go

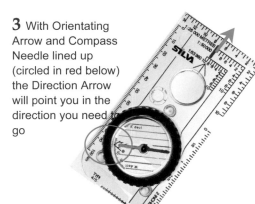

3. Pick up the compass and as long as the Compass Needle is lined up with the Orientating Arrow you can follow the Direction Arrow for your correct path.

GET LOST
170

The Lost Words of Cumbria

IN 2017 nature writer Robert Macfarlane and artist Jackie Morris teamed up to publish the book, *The Lost Words.* They had been alarmed by the decision of the Oxford Junior Dictionary to drop words like acorn, adder, bluebell, bramble and conker in favour of words like blog, broadband and celebrity. *The Lost Words* redressed the balance highlighting and celebrating some of the UK's nature words that were being neglected in the modern technological age. In this chapter we celebrate some of Cumbria's own 'lost words'; dialect words which are suffering from neglect. Where once Cumbrians used wath, lonning, trod or rake to distinguish different types of tracks, today most simply make do with 'path'. It's a shame and we lose a part of a rich heritage. So here are some of Cumbria's endangered words. We hope it rekindles interest in the likes of boggle, miry, gurn and Stinky Bob restoring them to our language.

GET LOST

171

Back End: Cumbria's fifth season. Cumbrians have long known that there are five seasons, not four. When you look at the year that way, the world begins to make more sense. This season was once an important time for Cumbrian farmers with 'back end' fairs being held to mark the occasion. It was a time to tidy up the farm and put the house in order before winter. To quote Millom poet Norman Nicholson: "It's that time when there are few leaves left on the trees, the days are at their shortest, and the weather at its darkest. Back End looks like it sounds: the dull, scraggy bits of the year".

Taking Bait.
Picture: Lilian Douglas Collection

Lately, some Cumbrians have simply defined 'back end' as another word for autumn but this is simply wrong.

Bait: Lunch. The term may have originated with the mining community and appears in other parts of Britain which have a history of mining. It is a word still commonly used in West Cumbria and usually refers to a simple 'takeaway' lunch such as sandwiches and drinks. See also *Clocks*.

Beck: One of a number of terms for a small stream. Just as there are numerous names for paths, so too are there several words for types of flowing water depending on their strength and whether you can cross them on foot.

Bield: A rough stone shelter on the fells, usually for geese. But this word has had something of an identity crisis. While most use it to describe a small drystone shelter on the fells for animals, it has also been used as the name for a trap for foxes; a trap that was baited with geese, hence its name. The ingenious beehive-shaped device would be used to snare foxes. You can still see the remains of some bields on the fells but they are no longer used to trap animals.

Bobs: B*stards On Bikes. A modern and humorous acronym for cyclists. We are on the side of all law-abiding and courteous road users be they on two wheels or four. Drive and cycle carefully on the county's narrow country lanes.

Boggle: A ghost. But actually a boggle was something more than just a ghost. It was defined by Jeremiah Sullivan in 1857 as "any shape, human, or animal, or composite, any unaccountable noise, may be a boggle". Each village appears to have had its own boggle. The Muncaster Boggle was said to be the ghost of a murdered girl; the Old Shepherd Boggle near Appleby was a whispy white troublesome figure that had to be laid by a Catholic priest; the Armboth Boggle was the spectre of a bride murdered on the eve of her wedding day; the Scallow Beck Boggle at Lamplugh walked like a dog but flew like an owl while the Dalehead Park Boggle appeared on one occasion in the form of a blazing fire, and on another in the form of a pile of manure! Boggles, it seems, can appear anywhere in any form. If you search on Google for Cumbria Boggles Map you will be directed to our map of the county's many boggles.

Bothy: A stone hut that can be used for shelther (by humans as opposed to a bield which is used by animals). The Mountain Bothies Association describes them as 'camping without a tent' and says "When going to a bothy, it is important to assume that there will be no facilities. No tap, no sink, no beds, no lights, and, even if there is a fireplace, perhaps nothing to burn. Bothies may have a simple sleeping platform, but if busy you

GET
LOST
173

might find that the only place to sleep is on a stone floor. You will need to make your own arrangement for water and should be aware that there may not be a suitable supply near the bothy. If there is no fire then on a cold night you may have trouble staying warm. The great majority of nights in Britain are on the cool side and remember that most bothies are up in the hills. Few bothies have toilet facilities apart from a spade and the advice is that you should walk at least a couple of hundred metres from the bothy and 60 metres from the water supply before excavations and evacuations commence." The Warnscale Head Bothy above

A clock lownd.

Buttermere is easily our favourite one, having the best 'view from a window' in the UK. See mountainbothies. org.uk for more information.

Cattle creep: A tunnel for cattle to pass through or under a road, railway or other obstacle. See also *smoot*.

Chitty: Small. As in chitty mouse (the name of our publishing company). We have a note of a path called Chitty Mouse Path at Cumwhinton but are unsure of its location. The word possibly originates from a medieval word chitte meaning the young or cub of an animal. A chitterling in some parts of the country refers to 'a very young child' (*The Lost Beauties of the English Language* by Charles MacKay, 1874).

Cleg: Horsefly.

Clock lownd: The dandelion clock. Lownd is 'calm, still' so it relates to the childhood game of blowing the dandelion head – the number of times blown

174

equating to the hours of the day. William Rollinson adds that in Cartmel, loand means 'quiet weather' (*The Cumbrian Dictionary*, William Rollinson 1997).

Clocks: Tea-break. Sometimes ten o'clocks after the hour at which the break was taken. A woman in Ennerdale told us how she used to take 'clocks' to her father and co-workers in the fields in the afternoon.

Corpse road: The path used in medieval times to carry the dead from a remote parish to the 'mother' church for burial. Until the 19th Century many mother churches held the monopoly on

Crag fast.

profitable burials and funerals so were reluctant to grant burial rights to other parishes. Many of the corpse roads or coffin paths still survive in Cumbria as public footpaths.

Crack: Gossip or conversation. Still commonly used in many

parts of Cumbria so if a Cumbrian says, "I've got some good crack for you" they may not be referring to illegal drug distribution!

Crag fast: Someone, or something, stuck on rocks. The term usually refers to sheep that have wandered onto rocky outcrops on the fells and have become 'crag fast' but often used for mountaineers or tourists who have become similarly stuck.

Crag rat: A mountaineer/ tourist. The name for someone who can speedily climb rock faces. It's also become an affectionate

GET LOST
175

term for tourists visiting the Lakes – the Cumbrian equivalent of the West Country term, 'grockles'.

Cuddy: Donkey. A term still used by some Cumbrian folk. Cuddy Lonning at Wigton was presumably one which had a donkey in it at some point in its history.

Cyak: Cake. Often used on signs outside cafes by proprietors desperate to show they're true Cumbrians.

Desire Path: Unofficial shortcuts. This is not a solely Cumbrian term but one used

A Desire Path.

by town planners to refer to footpaths created by people taking shortcuts and thus demonstrating where the footpath should go, not where it does. No matter how much a town planner may design pretty routes through an estate, most folk will take the shortest or most convenient 'desire path'.

Dobbie: A ghost. The Westmorland version of the term *boggle* (see above). It has been popularised by author J K Rowling who used the term for a house elf. In Cartmel there is a Dobbie Lane – the name arose from sightings of a mysterious will-o-the-wisp type light often seen in the lane.

Dyke: A hedge or wall. Different parts of Cumbria have subtle differences in the definition of a dyke but in general it refers to a hedge. Bob

Jackson in *Memories of a Lamplugh Farmer* (2018) wrote: "The hedge was usually growing on a dyke and had to be repaired by sodding the kest round the field ploughed out of lea which meant the dyke round the lea field was felled about every fifteen years". Hence he saw the dyke as the mound of earth on which the hedge grew. Kest also refers to a line of earth and is a term more frequently found in the north of the county.

Dykie: A hedge sparrow as opposed to a spuggy (a house sparrow).

Fat Man's Agony: A tight gap in a fence or rocks. There are a number of Fat Man's Agonys

A Fat Man's Agony.

in the Lake District including Scafell and Side Pike in Great Langdale but it's a term you will find used by Cumbrians to describe any narrow gap or gate (above).

Fell: A mountain. The term more frequently refers to the

level top of the mountain. The sport of fell running involves athletes running up (and back down) the fells. The King of the Fells is runner Joss Naylor who is now in his eighties but you are still likely to bump into him as he runs across the fells. Fell-bagging refers to the hobby of climbing as many fells as possible. Fell-baggers are those who keep count of the fells they have climbed.

Fox-fire: The phosphorescent glowing of the water in Morecambe Bay at night.

Gurn: To pull a funny face. Gurning championships

GET LOST
177

Champion gurner Anne Woods.

have been held in Egremont for over 750 years (since 1267) and are still held at the annual Crab Fair each September. Gurners put their head through a braffin (horse's collar) to gurn. One of the all-time great gurners is Tommy Mattinson who has won the title 14 times, earning him a place in the *Guinness Book of World Records*.

Champion female gurner is the late Anne Woods who won the ladies title 27 times.

Haaf-netting: A form of estuary fishing (catching salmon and sea trout) practised in the Solway Estuary and which may date back as far as Viking times. You can see haaf-netters at work on the shoreline but if you fancy having a go yourself, visit the Haaf Netters Fishing Association website at haafnettersfishing.co.uk.

Hefted: The term used to describe the ability of Herdwick sheep to remember their particular part of the fell; the heaf. That said Herdwicks are also famed for never being where they should be. Farmers often say that to put a Herdwick in a particular field you start by putting him two fields away from the one you want him to be in!

Jinny Howlet: An owl. Sometimes just Yowlet.

Kests: A sunken lane consisting of banks with hedges. Some good examples can be found near Burgh by Sands. See also *dyke*.

Kirk: A chapel or church.

La'al: Little, small. A word commonly used throughout Cumbria. Hence La'al Ratty is the little steam engine that runs between Ravenglass and Dalegarth in Eskdale The word can cause confusion. We once ordered two lattes at a cafe and a few minutes later the waitress brought over two la'al teas!

Liggin kessin: An upside-down sheep. When sheep fall or roll over accidentally they are usually unable to get back up the right way and remain liggin kessin. Please help any you see to return to the right way up. Just be aware that sheep can bite so steer clear of its head. A quick roll will enable him to jump up and carry on. Sheep will die if not righted.

Lonning: A country lane. But

Liggin kessin: An upside-down sheep.

a particular type of lane. A lonning is usually low-level and about half a mile long. Many are distinguished by a specific name as in West Lonning, Lovely Lonning, Bluebottle Lonning or Lovers Lonning. The name may have originated from the old word 'loan' meaning 'the quiet place by the farm'. This was where milk, eggs or other farm produce were sold so the lane

leading to the loan may have become the loaning. Sometimes spelt lonnin'. In the north-east it is spelt lonnen.

Lownd: Still/calm. "O for Billy Watson' lonnin of a lownd summer neeght!" (*Billy Watson' Lonnin*). Charles Mackay in *The Lost Beauties of the English Language* (1874) also records the word lown meaning still/calm and gives the example, "violets growing in the lown", which suggests it was also a noun for a quiet place, perhaps the same root as lonning. See also *clock lownd*.

Marra: Friend. Still widely used in

GET LOST
179

many parts of Cumbria.

Miry: Boggy, swampy, wet.

Occupation lane: A lane usually leading to land on the fells but crossing someone's private land. It gave the person with rights on the fell the ability to cross the private land.

Rake: A narrow path usually on a slope. Lady's Rake on the side of Walla Crag was – according to legend – where Lady Derwentwater made her escape after her husband's involvement in a failed Jacobite uprising. According to Robert Ferguson (1873)

GET LOST
180

A syke: Half stream, half path.

a rake could be climbed with a horse and cart but it's hard to see how that could have been achieved on Lady's Rake.

However it probably echoes a time when paths were defined by whether they could be accessed on horseback, with a cart or needed to be done on foot.

Rigg: A ridge.

Scree: Loose stones on the steep side of a fell. The Screes at Wasdale are perhaps the most famous. Be warned they are treacherous and people have died trying to cross them. Even if you feel you are capable of tackling them, it is a tedious and ankle-busting walk which is best avoided.

Slare: To amble, to walk slowly, to walk with no

particular purpose. This is the speed at which you should walk in Cumbria. It enables you to see the landscape and wildlife around you. There is an unhealthy obsession these days with 'doing' the Three Peaks or other challenges in 24 hours or X number of days. These folk have not 'done' anything but trample over the land and missed a golden opportunity to enjoy what Mother Nature has to offer. Don't run, don't walk, slare.

Smoot/smute: A hole in the bottom of a drystone wall for rabbits, hares or other small animals to get through. There are also larger ones (hogg holes) to allow sheep to wander from one field to another. See also

A smoot.

cattle creep. Smoot was an old Norse word meaning to creep into a hole.

Spink: A chaffinch.

Starving: Freezing cold. It can cause confusion when old newspaper reports talk of a body being found on the fells and that the person starved to death. This would usually mean they froze rather than died from lack of anything to eat.

Stee: A ladder or a vertical climb on a rockface.

Stinky Bob: Herb Robert. A charming little flower whose scent allegedly has the ability to repel midges and other insects. You crush the plant between your fingers and rub the juice onto your wrists and neck. It is part of the carrot family.

GET LOST
181

Stirk: A young heifer or bullock (usually between one and two years old). These can be very lively so give them a wide berth.

Stooks: The small stacks of corn that used to be found in fields in an age before the combine harvester. Technically, 12 sheaves of corn.

Syke: A small stream, particularly going through woods, which is also used as a footpath.

Tatie Pot: A Cumbrian delicacy. Herdwick

A trod: The most basic of paths.

mutton with black pudding and onions, topped with crisp brown potatoes and accompanied by pickled onions and a "la'al bit o' red cabbish" (William Rollinson). Tatie also meant small which may have reflected the usual small size of the portion in the individual pot. A quick Google will give you a rich variety of 'genuine' and 'original' Tatie Pot recipes.

Trod: The first and most basic type of footpath. Literally where sheep or cattle have trod. Humans undoubtedly follow and before long you have a full-blown path.

Wath: A crossing of an estuary. A most dangerous path to take. See page 143.

Yak: The oak tree as in Jack's Yak which proudly stood for 600 years on the Lowther Estate but sadly fell in a storm in January 2020. Yak kist – an oak chest.

• This is only a guide to some of the dialect and lost words from Cumbria; it is not intended to be comprehensive. Nor have we explored the origin of words. There are authors who try to do this but we recall an incident when we visited Dean, near Cockermouth, which showed the dangers of trying to explain the origin of words or place names. At Dean there is a road

Jack's Yak oak tree which sadly collapsed in January 2020. Grid Ref: NY525 242.

(indeed field) called America Field. We speculated this might be because of the area's links with Quakerism or perhaps even the west coast of Cumbria's slavery connection. When we asked an elderly lady she

pointed to a nearby beck and said: "It's a village joke – you have to cross water to get to it."

GET LOST

183

Get lost in a good book

Further reading for your enjoyment

Fairies

Seeing Fairies by Marjorie T Johnson. Published by Anomalist Books. Reports of fairies in modern times including the Borrowdale fairy sightings.

Magical Folk by Simon Young and Ceri Houlbrook. An informed account of the fairy tradition in Britain and Ireland. Published by Gibson Square.

Strange Lands by Andrew L Paciorek. A wonderfully-illustrated book detailing all the boggles, dobbies and other-worldly creatures you are in constant danger of encountering.

Local histories

Too many to mention but here are just a few…

Caldbeck: A Special Part of Lakeland by Tony Vaux. A

GET LOST 184

comprehensive history of this lovely village.

The Gosforth District by Dr C A Parker. First published in 1904 and reprinted by Michael Moon in 2009.

A History of Warton Parish by John Lucas. Details the history in the early 18th Century. Published with additional notes by Andy Denwood in 2017.

Sand Pilot of Morecambe Bay by Cedric Robinson (former Queen's Guide to Morecambe Bay). One of a number of fascinating books by Mr Robinson.

A Literary Guide to the Lake District by Grevel Lindop. Details links of authors and their books to the Lake District.

Grasmere: A History in 55½ Buildings by Grasmere History Group. A wonderful tour of the village and its past.

Special thanks to all those who have published little histories of their village or church which proves invaluable for local information.

Footpaths

Roads and Tracks of the Lake District by Paul Hindle. Published by Cicerone Press. Dr Hindle is the definitive guide to the history of the county's paths.

GET LOST 185

An Illustrated Guide to The Packhorse Bridges of the Lake District by Michael Hartwell. Published by Ernest Press. There are a number of books detailing the packhorse bridges in the county but this is one of the nicest.

The Lake District traditions

Jack's Yak by Keith Richardson (Photos by Val Corbett). An exploration of the ancient trees of Cumbria.

The Folklore of the Lake District by Marjorie Rowling. Published by Batsford 1976. Remains the

GET LOST 186

go-to book for Lake District folklore.

Life and Tradition in the Lake District by William Rollinson – or any book by Mr Rollinson.

Springs of Living Waters - the holy wells of North Cumbria by Fr John Musther. Published 2015. An almost complete guide to the locations and state of holy wells in the county.

Odd Yarns of English Lakeland by William T Palmer. Published by Skeffington & Son, 1914. And any book by Mr Palmer who appears to have written dozens of books about the Lake District in the early 20th Century.

Walking

Any books by Vivienne Crow, Mark Richardson and Beth Pipe – but there are countless other worthy authors of walks in the Lake District.

The Gentle art of Tramping by Stephen Graham. This 1927 classic has been republished by Bloomsbury Reader.

Any books by Alfred Wainwright. These are kept updated by Frances Lincoln publishers.

Dialect

The Dialect of Cumberland by Robert Ferguson. First published in 1873, now available as a reprint.

The Cumbrian Dictionary by William Rollinson. First published in 1997.

The Lost Beauties of the English Language - Charles Mackay. First published in 1874 and reprinted in 1987. It is available from second-hand bookshops.

Websites

www.heritagepaths.co.uk: For Scottish paths. A wonderful website.

www.lownestfarm.co.uk/olden/dialect.htm – for Cumbrian

dialect words.

www.normannicholson.org: The Norman Nicholson Society

Gridreferencefinder.com: Type in a grid reference or a post code and it will show you on a map (even an OS map). Or find a location and it will show the grid reference.

Bing.com/maps - One up on Google maps as you can choose to view as an OS map.

ruslandhorizons.org: Rusland Horizons: A project to celebrate the heritage, habitats and wildlife of the Rusland Valley.

solwayshorewalker.wordpress.

com: Solway Shore-walker. Ann Lingard is your guide to this stunning part of Cumbria.

www.lctrust.co.uk: Website of the Lancaster Canal Trust.

This is just a selection of works from our ever-growing bookshelves and we know we will have to apologise in the future for missing out inadvertently the good works of friends and colleagues. But wander into any of the county's wonderful independent bookshops and they will advise you on local books to suit your needs.

GET LOST 187

Index

Printed by H&H Reeds
of Penrith

15039900248
Printed on Carbon Captured paper